HOW TO GET THE BEST IT JOB EVER!

Simple and easy techniques which you can implement today - to make sure you get the job of your dreams!

Richard Morgan

HOW TO GET THE BEST IT JOB EVER!

First paperback edition printed 2012 in the United Kingdom.

A catalogue record for this book is available from the British Library.

ISBN 978-1-907308-21-5

For more copies of this book, please email:
orders@howtogetthebestitjobever.com

Published by Compass Publishing
www.Compass-Publishing.com

Designed and Set by The Book Refinery Ltd
www.TheBookRefinery.com

Printed in Great Britain

CONTENTS

Introduction

What is This Book About?

It can seem very hard to find a great job in IT, it's easy to blame the economy, but this doesn't explain why some people—who are no better educated or talented than the less successful ones among us—are landing their dream jobs every day. So, what's going on?

The differences between these fortunate and less fortunate people lie in the ways they go about trying to get their dream job. The purpose of this book, therefore, is to show you how you can jump off the merry-go-round of applying for jobs and getting nowhere, and instead attract job offers without ever having to apply for a job again. You'll also discover how to attract job offers that PAY MORE, that give you MORE time to do the things you enjoy, and that allow you to GO FURTHER in IT, quickly and easily. What's more, you can achieve ALL THIS by following my simple, 3-step process.

By the end of this book you'll realise that landing your dream IT job is actually pretty simple. You just need to follow *'the 3-step process'*, understand what the world looks like today, and work out where you fit into it. Frustration and demotivation will become things of the past; instead, you'll enjoy the process of job hunting as much as the end results of finding that perfect job!

Who is This Book For?

If any of the following sound like you, then this book is for you:

- ✓ I'm applying for hundreds of jobs and getting NO responses
- ✓ I'm getting interviews but not getting job offers
- ✓ I'm prepared to do something different but I don't know what
- ✓ I'd love to get off the merry-go-round of short term dead end contracts

If you follow the 3 step process outlined in this book, you will get the job you want, guaranteed. You will need to follow the whole sequence to achieve this, but the good news is there are lots of quick tricks that will help you to....

- ➲ Get more interviews
- ➲ Create the right first impressions
- ➲ Get job offers

None of the ideas in this book are complicated, in fact, they're all really simple. But you will need to do some things differently; to step outside your comfort zone; to be positive, open, and able to show your value to others.

If you think that by reading this book (or any book for that matter) but doing nothing differently will make you the next Mark Zuckerberg, then please save your time and effort and put the book down!

And if you think that what you're currently doing (in regards to job seeking) is right, then great you don't need to read any further.

On the other hand, if you ARE prepared to do things differently, please read on.

But please don't just read it, take ACTION!

I ask only two things:

1. Be open to new ideas
2. Be prepared to do something different

If you are NOT prepared to do things differently and roll up your sleeves, then you will always struggle to find a job that fits, always be flitting from one to job to another, and you certainly won't find yourself the best IT job ever.

An interesting story...

I want to share with you a particular experience I had recently, because it was what prompted me to write this book at precisely the time I did...

Not long ago, I was retained to recruit for a Helpdesk Support post based in Central London. Over a thousand people applied for this job. Of course, I couldn't speak to a fraction of the people who applied, so I couldn't give them feedback. And I knew for a fact that 99.9% of the people who applied would be disappointed. I also recognised a lot of the names, they were the same people who applied whenever I had these types of jobs posted.

So, I put together an email saying **3 things** and sent it to everyone who applied:

Due to the volume of applications, I wasn't able to give individual feedback. I had over a thousand people apply but the client needed a shortlist in 2 days, which had been sent and they appointed someone based on that.

I was putting together a free webinar where I would explain what the market was like and how to best go about getting a great job. I also explained I'd never done a webinar before and if anyone knew any software or how to set up a webinar, to please get in touch.

I also asked, *"If there is one question you could ask that would help you get ahead in your job search, what would it be?"*

I had a lot of response to that email:

To point one, the response was: *"Thanks for letting me know but I'm perfect for that job and I don't understand why I haven't got it."* (Often a lot more aggressive than that, I realise people are frustrated!)

To point two: Lots of people thought it was a good idea and wanted to register an interest in the webinar.

But, interestingly, do you know how many offered to help me setup the webinar? Not one.

To point three: The question almost everyone asked was *"what buzz words do I need on a CV to make recruiters take notice?"*

These responses to my three questions made me realise two things: Firstly—and quite understandably—job seekers do not understand why companies use recruiters or how recruitment works; and, secondly, the reason they have yet to find a great IT job is that they're going about job hunting in entirely the wrong way.

Now, because the fact that not a single person offered to

help me set up my webinar is so important in the context of this book, we'll be looking at this in more detail later in the book.

Here, though, let's look at the dominant response to question 3: *"What buzz words do I need on a CV to make recruiters take notice?"* People generally believed that the quality of their CV is the most important factor in getting shortlisted.

How important are CVs?

Everyone thinks CVs are important—they are—but they're not as important as other things that I'll be covering in this book.

In brief, a CV is a document you use to get an interview.

To get interviews, your CV needs to have two things:

Proof that you can do the specific job you are applying for. That proof doesn't need to be commercial experience, but it does need to be there in the very first paragraph. The one question everyone who has a job in IT has worked out the answer to is the 'no commercial experience' question.

It also needs to sell!

This is as much detail as I can go into in this book about CVs. If you need more help on how to write a killer CV, visit www.brightstarttraining.com/itentrylevel

However, let me point out that having a great CV with all

the latest 'buzz words' is, in short, NOT going to get you the job of your dreams. *The 3 step process* that I am about to share with you will. BUT you need to take action, do the things that I suggest, and be open to a new way of thinking. If you do these things then I can guarantee that you will be setting yourself up for success and, most importantly, be in demand. And being in demand is the key to getting your dream job in IT

Enjoy the book, and I have created a fantastic online video programme especially for you that covers everything in this book in much more detail, giving you access to setting you up for success on your pursuit of your IT job and helps you implement all of the tactics that I share with you, *enabling you to get* the best IT job ever. (Please see back of book for more details of how to get access to this programme.)

Good luck. And I wish you all the best in your job seeking.

Richard

Richard Morgan.

SECTION 1

- **Introduction to the 3-step process**
- **The truth about recruitment agencies**
- **Step 1 - Specialise**
- **Step 2 - Attract**
- **Using social media to find real time opportunites**
- **Step 3 - Go further**

SECTION 1

An Introduction to 'The 3-Step Process'

To introduce *'The 3-Step Process'* to getting your ideal job in IT, I'd like to ask you a question:

Have you ever wondered why some people never have to apply for jobs?

We all know these people; they're the ones that:-

- ✓ Get every job they're interviewed for
- ✓ Earn more money
- ✓ Work on exciting projects

They never have to apply for jobs; they get 'head hunted', make choices, and decide their own future.

In my job I've spoken to a lot of these people. Do you know what makes these people different? A lot less than you would imagine.

Are these people naturally gifted? No.

Do they come from privileged backgrounds? No.

Do they have the same insecurities as you? Yes.

So, what does make these people different?

It's simple. They decided to **specialise** in an area they

enjoyed, they worked hard at building skills in that area, and they stuck at it.

Simple? Yes!

Easy? No!

It takes hard work but it is worth it. Below I'm going to tell you about someone we all know and his story exemplifies the point I am making. Now, this example is not someone in the IT arena, but it clearly shows how powerful specialising can be. You can do the same and discover one of the quickest ways to get the IT job of your dreams.

An example of this process at work:

His recent problems aside, the most successful sportsman of our generation is Tiger Woods. We all know that Tiger Woods was '**born to be the best golfer**' of all time, has a **'freak talent'**, and is more **'naturally gifted'** than any other golfer. Don't we?

There's just one problem with all of these statements: *They're not true!* Any budding golfer wanting to follow in Tiger Wood's footsteps probably wouldn't get very far if he or she thought about Tiger's success in these terms. Why? Because the reasons here do not allow any room for the fact that we can learn to be better golfers (in the same way that we can learn to be better at pretty much anything we have potential for).

Let's break down briefly what Tiger Woods did:
He **specialised** in golf (at a very young age). He didn't try tennis or baseball in case he didn't make it at golf,

in fact he didn't play other sports. He found a sport that he enjoyed and was good at, and he stuck at it. He **practiced**. A lot! As a result of this practice he developed his skills and began to improve.

Because he practiced hard and started early, he began to attract attention. He was famously on TV at a very young age. People took an interest in him. He kept practicing and kept getting better. He attracted more attention and started to get invited to the best tournaments.

Because he attracted this attention, successful people and the best coaches wanted to work with him. The best coaching in the world helped him go even further. He started to win tournaments, and he ended up with the best job ever.

Was it easy? Absolutely not! He overcame obstacles that most of us would have given up at.

Let's take another look at the statements we made earlier:

- **'Born to be the best golfer'?** No, he wasn't. He wasn't from a privileged background and wasn't even allowed to play at some of the top golf courses in the US. The biggest tournament in the world is the US Masters, they had to change the rules to allow him to play.

- '**Freak talent**'? No! He just found something he really enjoyed, was good at, stuck at it, and practiced harder than anyone else.

- '**Naturally gifted**'? Again, no. He had practiced his skills and was obviously very good but there were others who were just as good as him. When Tiger was the best young amateur in the US, the best young amateur in Europe was Gordon Sherry. (Who? Isn't that something Grandma drinks at Christmas?)

Tiger Woods followed the 3-step process that I'm going to share with you in more detail throughout the following sections.

The 3-Step Process:

➲ Specialise;
➲ Attract;
➲ Go further.

As a result of following this simple 3-step process, Tiger Woods ended up with the best job ever. And you can do the same.

Now, before we get into the 3-step process, I'm quickly going to explain why looking for jobs the old fashioned way won't get you your dream job in IT I'll also quickly explain the role of the recruiter so that you have a full picture of how that side of 'job hunting' is done and why approaching recruitment companies is probably not your best option. It makes for interesting reading!

The Truth About Recruitment Agencies

Why traditional job seeking methods don't work anymore.

If you have yet to find your dream job in IT, you're probably going about job hunting in the same way that most other people do: Searching job ads on the internet and applying for the jobs you're interested in, either directly to the employers or via recruitment agencies. *"Yes, but these are the only ways to get the perfect job, aren't they?"* I hear you say. The answer is a most definite NO! Blindly sending off your CV to employers and recruitment agencies will NOT land you your ideal job.

Why?

To help you understand why this typical way of job searching is the worst strategy you can use, I'm going to give you an insider's look at what recruiters do and how they work.

The 4 *'Insider Secrets'* To Recruiters:

1. **What recruiters do**
2. **Why employers use recruiters**
4. **How recruiters work**
5. **Where the majority of jobs come from**

Once you're armed with this inside information that I'm about to share, you'll then be able to invest your time and energy in doing things that *will help you* to find your ideal job. And I'm going to show you exactly what those things are in the remaining sections.

1. What recruiters do;

It's important to define the role of a recruiter and how that relates to you and your job search. What I mean by 'recruiters' is third party recruiters (recruitment consultancies or agencies).

The recruiter's role is possibly very different to what you think, but it is very simple: **Recruiters are paid by their clients to find candidates and people for their clients' jobs.** Recruitment is a very cut-throat environment. If recruiters don't find people they won't have jobs themselves for very long. It is also very competitive, recruiters need to find the right people for their jobs.

Now, it would be great if recruiters were there to coach; to provide feedback; to provide lots of things. They're not. Their job is to find someone for their client's job, it's as simple as that.

2. Why employers use recruiters;

Companies use recruiters like myself for two reasons, and two reasons only:

1. Insufficient time;
2. The need to identify 'specialists' that are not otherwise readily available.

Let's look at these two points in more detail, along with what they mean in terms of the success or otherwise of your applications...

Insufficient time.

The first reason companies use recruiters is because they don't have the time to go through the recruitment process themselves but they need someone in post immediately. If a company needs to have someone on site in a couple of days, they simply don't have the time to go through the process of advertising in the paper, buying all the different adverts, and dealing with the hundreds of applications they receive in response to their adverts.

So, for example, imagine a company approaches me one Wednesday afternoon saying, *"I need someone on the helpdesk by first thing on Monday morning."* In an urgent situation like this, I would advertise the post on the job boards, get all of the responses in, and then start talking to people. If there are people on my database I know who are active and who I know are good, I'll send them over for interview; if not, I'll start talking to people.

Now, if you were among the applicants responding to this job posting in this situation, you probably wouldn't even be approached for interview. This could be the case even if you had the best CV out of all of the applicants for this post.

There are 2 reasons for this:-

1. Helpdesk support positions are highly competitive because they are generally regarded as the entry point for a career in IT I'd expect to

receive around 1000 CVs for a job like this;

2. In an urgent situation like this, the recruiter simply does not have the time to look, in depth, at all of the applications they've received. I deal with situations like this by talking to people in my database and, when I have five good ones, I put them on the shortlist and send them over to the employer. Now, if you're lucky and you're one of those five good ones then that's great, but that's pure luck. Among those 1000 applicants there are probably many who can do the job, but they're not going to get the chance to do the job because urgency of time means I'm never going to speak to them.

Identifying 'Specialists'.

The second reason companies use recruiters is because they need specialist talent that isn't readily available. What I mean by 'not being readily available' is that if a company bought an advert in the evening paper, or bought an advert on one of the online job boards, they wouldn't get anyone responding to it.

In IT, companies often want to employ someone who is skilled at doing something very specific. For example, imagine a company needs someone who can come in and administer their email systems. The email system that is used in most companies is Microsoft Exchange. So, that company might be looking for someone who is a specialist in Microsoft Exchange. Another company might need someone who is a specialist in SQL databases; another, a

C# Developer; and another, a Storage/Unix Administrator. These are all examples of IT jobs that require very specific skills. They are also examples of IT jobs that are high in demand but low in competition. We'll be looking at the advantages of applying for jobs like this later on.

Can you now see why trying to land a job by sending in your CV to a company or recruitment agency is not going to be very effective, especially where the job you're applying for is very competitive (generic)? The odds are stacked against you.

Consider applications to companies and enrolling with recruitment companies as only two of a number of ways to get your dream job...

3. How recruiters work;

Because recruiters often have to find employees quickly, and competition for graduate / entry level jobs is fierce, it should be clear that you're unlikely to find that dream job by approaching recruitment companies alone.

In fact, I would go so far as to say that without having two years of experience you shouldn't be using recruitment agencies at all! The reason for this is because—at least for graduate or entry level jobs such as the helpdesk Support role—it's very difficult to prove yourself. Without having worked on a helpdesk, how easy is it to prove that you're great at working on a helpdesk?

Not easy at all.

And when you combine that with the level of competition for these jobs, what are your chances of getting the job?

Pretty impossible.

Similarly, neither should you put all your efforts into blindly sending out your CV in response to every job advert you see that you think you could do.

How many jobs are found as a result of recruiters and job advertisements?

By 'putting all your eggs in one basket', you're also unlikely to land your dream job because of another reason. And that reason is because only a very small percentage of jobs in the UK are advertised by employers or sourced through recruitment agencies. And when I say very small, I mean ***very small!***

It's quite common for people to think that putting your CV with recruitment agencies and responding directly to job adverts are the only ways to go about job hunting; but, in actual fact, only 20% of all available jobs in the UK are found by responding to job adverts. This means that if you're using recruiters and company job adverts as your only sources for finding a job, you are ignoring 80% of all of the available jobs out there.

And if you're relying solely upon recruitment agencies, you are ignoring a whopping 92% of all of the available jobs out there. (Of course, this raises the question of where the vast majority of jobs do come from and we'll be looking at this very shortly).

Two ways to approach recruitment agencies;

Now, I'm not saying that it's always a bad idea to approach recruitment agencies; however, if you do then you need to do it in a certain way:-

1. If you're applying for a helpdesk job—or any other generic (non-specialist) job where there are going to be over a thousand other people applying—you need to ***be different*** (in a good way of course).

To give you an example of how *you can be different*, I'd like you to think back to the example I gave in the Introduction where I'd asked for technical support for my webinar.

Did I need help? No. I'm pretty technical and can work it out for myself (although it would've been nice and would have saved me time).

Did I need to offer the webinar? No.

How many other recruiters have offered a webinar when you've applied for a job?

Why did I do it? I knew I had valuable information that could help and thought I might make some new contacts, and who knows what would come from that (as it turns out, a book).

Lots of people were open to the idea of me spending *my time* giving them this valuable information (for free), but *no one* thought of spending their time helping me do this.

If they had, would it have got them that specific job? No, it had already gone. But what about the next time that job came up? I suspect my first call would have been to the person who had offered me help with my webinar.

Stand out from the crowd, *differentiate yourself!*

2. When you're applying for jobs via recruiters (or in direct response to job advertisements), you need to bear in mind that a company will only offer you a job and pay the recruiter's fee if they're convinced that you can do the job. Employers don't like to take risks; they don't like to be out on a limb. And if a company has a thousand people applying for a job, they don't need to take risks, they can just be very safe and go for the people who can *prove* they can do the job.

As I mentioned earlier in this section, unless you have commercial experience, you'll find it very difficult to ***prove your ability*** in helpdesk support and other graduate-level entry jobs; however, you *will* be able to prove your ability in software development and other specialist jobs. How? By developing some websites, by creating applications and getting them on the App Store, by creating anything that is software- based.

This then *proves* your ability

So, only turn to recruiters such as myself if you can ***differentiate yourself*** and ***prove*** that you have the specialist skills needed to do a particular job. You'll stand a much better chance of finding a job if you can say to the recruitment company, "*this is what I can do, I can develop x, y, z technologies; take a look at my online portfolio.*" Because specialising is **SO important**—it's the first and most important step in my 3-step sequence to landing your perfect job—I talk about it in detail in the next section.

4. Where the vast majority of jobs come from;

I mentioned earlier that only 20% of all available jobs in the UK are found by responding to job adverts (directly or via recruiters). This begs the question, "*Where do the remaining 80% of jobs come from?*"

➲ **From referrals and recommendations.**

In other words, the vast majority of jobs (the ones that aren't advertised) go to people who employers know.

But in this day and age, it's not about who your Dad knows or about what school you went to; it's about **networking**—*developing relationships*—with people who you can get in touch with directly. I've said a couple of times already that you need to be open minded, prepared to be different, and creative. This is where you need to do it: Invest your time in building relationships (if you don't believe me, do it alongside sending out hundreds of CV's, I know which method will be more successful in the end). How? You'll find out later on in the book.

Open the door to the hidden job market which shows you how to identify real time job opportunities by accessing my online video course covers see back of book for more details on how you can gain *instant access* to this little known information. Or simply visit www.brightstarttraining.com/itpro

Summary

I hope that, by now, you realise that a sole reliance on the traditional (old fashioned) way of applying for jobs doesn't work anymore. Sending out hundreds of CVs or loading your CV on Job Boards and hoping for a response will not get you a great job in IT

Instead, you need to:-

- ✓ Differentiate yourself;
- ✓ Prove your ability;
- ✓ Invest your time in *building relationships* and *networking*.

Understanding what recruiters do and how recruiters work will help you understand that using them isn't your most effective way of getting your dream job. Instead you need to differentiate yourself, prove that you can do the job, and network. The 3-Step Process shows you how to do all of those things, so let's get cracking with the first step; **Specialise!**

STEP 1 - Specialise

If there is only one message you take away from this book, it needs to be this; SPECIALISE!

If you think about it, specialists are everywhere...

Where do you go and buy your clothes? The same shop as your parents? I doubt it. It's going to be a shop (or shops) that sell exactly, and only, the types of clothes that you like and want.

Likewise, when you have toothache, do you go to your GP? No, (at least I hope not) you go to your dentist.

Why You Need to be a Specialist

Specialising is *going to be more critical than ever before* for people to succeed because of the way in which the world of work and IT is changing. The way your parents and their parents thought about careers is not the way you should think about yours.

My grandparents' generation worked with the same company from the day they left school to the day they retired. Sometimes (if they worked hard) they could progress in the company, earn more, and take on more responsibility. That changed by the time my parents' generation started work and whilst, when they started out, they probably thought they would have a 'job for life', in reality they had three or four 'careers'. And, in this day and age, working hard, being enthusiastic, and being committed aren't advantages, they are requirements. Everyone does these things, so they're expected and taken for granted. The advantages are in **thinking differently**, **spotting opportunities**, and *taking advantages* of these opportunities.

I've had 5 jobs, have run 3 businesses, have clients across the world, and am writing this book from the south coast of Spain. You'll probably have a lot more than 5 jobs and you will have (if you take my advice) the opportunity to work and travel like never before; but you will not have a long career with one or two employers.

In the future, jobs will be 'on demand'. And by that I mean they'll be 'as and when needed', rather than permanent positions. So, instead of having an 'office administrator' who will try and complete all my tasks for me, I have specific people who are trained specifically for the jobs I need looking after. For example, I have a great PA, a top class book keeper to manage all of my contracts and accounts, a team of people who answer my phone to make sure I never miss a call, and a great web developer who designs my web sites. I could go on... But the point is that I 'buy in' services when I need them; I hire 'on demand'.

Could I afford to employ all of these people permanently? No. I wouldn't have enough work for them to employ them all of the time. But this new model allows me to work with experts; people who are great at doing specific things —**specialists**— when and where I need them.

The IT industry is changing, *and the way you think about your career needs to change too.*

In the IT industry we see changes constantly; in the next few years we will see even more.

Why?

The reason is not entirely down to the recessions we've seen in recent years; it's because jobs, and job markets, are changing. If we think about what the world is like today, everything is online and very, very, data driven. And all of that data must be organised in databases. When the economy recovers, the old jobs won't be coming back but they will be replaced by other jobs. The new jobs are going to be online-type jobs; they're going to be developing software, managing data, and working in the Cloud.

Don't just take my word for it here, take a few minutes to go and have a look at http://www.prnewswire.com/ and what it says about the Best Jobs of 2012.

What's the Number 1 job?

➲ Software Engineer!

"But I don't develop software" I hear you say.

How long does it take to learn the skills to develop an App or a Web page? In fact, how long does it take to develop the skills to learn any programming language? Not as long as you think, and certainly well within 6 months.

Think about it, the next time you're going for a job what would you rather have, a CV and a thousand others as competitors, or an App in the AppStore as proof of what you can do? (The AppStore is only one example, all of the other platforms have them, for example, BlackBerry, Google (Android), and Microsoft).

The brilliant thing about this is that it is happening all over the world; so, whilst some opportunities are disappearing new ones are appearing all the time.

"But what if I don't like or want to develop software?"

This is only one example, there are lots of other ways of niching into a particular area of popularity. You just need to be creative and different. So, if you're not into writing code, there will be something else. It may be that you're very data-driven and you want to manage databases; or maybe you think online backups are for you. It doesn't really matter but, whichever area you decide to specialise in, the key message is look at where the demand is — assuming you have the background knowledge and interest in that area—it's not a bad place to specialise.

If you want some more help with this go to www.brightstarttraining.com/itentrylevel and enter your name and email address. I've put together a toolkit that will help you. There will be something that suits you where there's demand.

Why Specialising is Critical

When I advise job seekers to specialise, I normally get 3 **objections** (excuses?)

1. No employer will give me a chance as I don't have any commercial experience.

2. Recruiters aren't interested in me as I don't have commercial experience.

3. I can't afford to specialise, because it's hard to get a job I need to apply for as many jobs as possible.

On the face of it, I understand these thoughts. In the past I've felt the same; I've experienced the same frustrations, the same rejection, and the same despair.

But let's take a look at the first two points above:

1 & 2 - no commercial experience:

Do you know one thing every single person working in IT has in common? They have worked out how to answer the 'no commercial' experience question.

HOW?

They have proven that they have ***valuable knowledge in a particular area*** without having had commercial experience.

Let's look at an example...

Five years ago, who had heard of Apps? No one. The Apple App Store had just opened and smart phones were just being released.

Since then hundreds of thousands of Apps have been created, across all platforms. These Apps weren't from the big games developers. They were from small companies; individuals being creative and different, and selling their work globally. In fact, only just recently, the Angry Birds game has been valued for listing on the stock exchange at over 5 billion dollars, not bad for a game that tries to knock things over with

> angry birds!
>
> Companies that were started from bedrooms have expanded and gone on to make millions of pounds by people who are as young as 17, 18 and in their early twenties. As well as the big success stories, there are now thousands and thousands of technical IT people working in this market.

If you've approached a company that specialises in developing apps for smart phones and you have developed an app on your own initiative, what does that say to a future employer?

Do you think they will care how much commercial experience you have, or do you think they will care how good your app is?

When employers or recruitment agencies are looking to hire and they have applicants to consider, who do you think stands the best chance of getting the job, the person who has taken the time to develop an app, or the person who is just sending out CVs saying they want a job developing apps?

I've used apps as an example but this can apply to web design or web development and many other areas. But, as I mentioned a moment ago, what if developing code (or web design) isn't your thing? This is where you need to be creative and think about how you can prove to a future employer that you have the skills they're looking for.

So, if writing code isn't your thing, how about creating a series of 'how to' videos on YouTube, or setting up a blog to help solve peoples' technical problems, or creating a database that you can show employers?

Think about what you can do to stand out from the crowd. Put yourself in the employer's shoes who would you hire? The person who has just sent you a CV or the person who has gone to a lot of effort to ***do something*** positive? (Remember, of course, that if it's your thing, it shouldn't be a big effort, it should be fun). I know who I would hire, the one with the passion, energy, and love for what they do, *every* time.

Now that we've dealt with the '***no commercial experience***' problem, let's look at the final objection I get to specialising:

3. I can't afford to specialise

Really?

Let's analyse this statement by having a look at two jobs that differ in terms of the level of specialist expertise involved:

1. Helpdesk support;
2. Graduate / Junior entry level software developer.

What should be clear is that job Number 1 is the job that involves the least amount of specialist IT skills, whereas job Number 2 is the job that involves more specialist expertise. Now, what do you think your chances are of getting each of these jobs?

In actual fact, you have a 1,000 to 1 shot in scenario 1 but a 25 to 1 chance of getting the job in scenario 2. So, if you go with scenario 2 then you have a far better chance of landing the IT job of your dreams.

There's also another big advantage of going for the more specialist job: Specialist jobs pay more! Going back to the two scenarios above, the first scenario will only pay you £16,000 a year; the second scenario will pay you £25,000 a year.

So, which one do you want? Which scenario do you want to invest your time in? I'm betting it's scenario 2. If it was me I think I'd spend some of my time learning to develop some software....

The point here is that specialists earn more money; they pick and choose the contracts they want, and they are ***in demand.***

These specialists earn MORE money, THEY pick and choose the contracts, and they are IN DEMAND!

Do you want to see more proof? Go to http://www.itjobswatch.co.uk/. The information you will find is real time and up to date. Try a few searches on that web page for the following:-

- 1st Line
- 2nd Line
- 3rd Line
- C#
- PHP
- Ruby on Rails
- Commvault

Have a look at the difference in pay rates for the same job on a permanent basis and on a contract basis. The more specialist the skills, the more they pay. Look also at the number of jobs that are available. What I find interesting is that there are a lot more of the jobs that pay well. How can that be? Simple, specialist skills are in demand. Companies want people with specialist skills but there isn't the supply of those people and this drives up the salaries that companies are prepared to pay. Those companies then start coming to *look for you*. You stop having to send out hundreds of CV's and you start getting lots of calls and job offers. Your problem will then be picking the jobs that look interesting, that are the most fun, and that pay the most money.

Which job would you rather have? Which one is going to get you what you want, and get it faster?

I hope you're starting to see how crucial it is to specialise...

Why 'Apple' is the market leader.

Why are there huge queues outside the Apple Store when other electrical shops are struggling and disappearing? Because they specialise. They don't try to be 'all things to all people', they focus on an area so that they are able to deliver a high quality service.

Now, does this mean that there is no room whatsoever for electrical shops that stock generalist products?

No, they still have customers and there is still some demand for them.

But ask yourself this question?

"Why is one of them the most valuable brand in the world and why are the rest struggling to stay afloat?"

Which company would you rather be?

Can you now see that the *"I can't afford to specialise"* argument has very shaky foundations? The fact is that you can't afford NOT to specialise. Over the last 10 years I've spoken to hundreds of people who have proven this to be true; sadly, though, thousands will not change, or for some reason they don't think it applies to them. They're making a big mistake.

Does specialising take a lot of effort? Of course it does. But if you do specialise you will stand out and you will get the job you want.

How do you decide which area to specialise in?

I've already talked about how important it is to specialise in an area that's in demand. At the same time, though, there's something else you need to bear in mind when you're deciding which area of IT to specialise in:

➲ **Do something you enjoy!**

You'll often hear people saying *"do something you love doing and the rewards will come."* And this is, generally speaking, true. Now, I'm not going to bore you with lots of scientific evidence showing that people are happier and more successful in jobs that are intrinsically satisfying. Suffice to say that there's a lot of evidence that when people enjoy what they do for a living, they reap more rewards—financial and psychological—than when they do not enjoy what they do.

The key message here is *choose something that you enjoy without thinking too much about pay.* Provided the job has prospects, your initial salary should not be a major factor in your decision to take that job or not. When we do something for monetary, as opposed to intrinsic, gain we are less motivated in that job and have lower job satisfaction (and sometimes also lower life satisfaction). If David Beckham and Richard Branson were doing what they do only for the money, both would have retired many years ago. Instead, these highly successful, and very rich, business people are highly successful and rich because they get immense intrinsic (internal) satisfaction from their work.

So, without a doubt, if you are going to have a great career in anything it needs to be something you enjoy doing. But it also has to be something that suits your ability and personality traits. I love singing; I do it all the time and enjoy a night out at Karaoke. Ask any of my friends and they'll tell you how enthusiastic I am and how much I enjoy it. But I also know that I'm never going to be a professional. There's one simple reason for this, I have a terrible singing voice.

It's the same with work. It needs to be something you enjoy but it also needs to be something you're suited to. So, while we can all learn to get better at something (just as Tiger Woods learned to get better at golf), there needs to be some ability there that we can develop. I don't think it would be too contentious for me to say that Tiger Woods is more able at golf than Eddie 'The Eagle' Edwards is at skiing!

Summary

Being able to demonstrate your ability to be innovative, and overcoming the 'no commercial' experience objection (by developing something), is a smart tactic to implement. Include a speciality in your application and you're well on your way to getting your dream job in IT.

➲ **Specialising is THE key factor for success.**

It's the one process that I really want you to take away from this book. Not sure what to specialise in? It's quite simple, choose something that you're passionate about AND that you're suited too. Without specialising, you will just get a job...

Specialise; the key to earning more and being in demand.

Want to learn how to differentiate yourself from the competition and distinguish yourself in a tough market place? Then see my online video programme which goes into much more detail of how to accomplish this. Visit www.brightstarttraining/itpro for more details.

STEP 2 - Attract

You'll remember that, earlier in this book, I talked about why the traditional job-seeking strategy—blindly sending out CVs and application forms in response to job adverts—no longer works. You might remember that the main reason for this is that most people find their jobs in a much less formal way, by building connections and developing relationships with people.

➲ What I'm talking about here is networking.

As we'll see, networking can be extremely powerful when it's done properly because it enables you to ***attract*** offers. In other words, employers approach *you* instead of you having to approach *them*. If you can change your job-finding mind-set from 'job hunting' to 'job attracting', you'll get ahead in IT much more quickly and much more easily. And wouldn't you agree that networking and making friends with people is far more fun than sending out a mountain of job applications every week?

The idea that making new contacts and developing relationships can help people to get ahead in their careers isn't new; however, how we do these things has changed dramatically in recent years. In this day and age, it's easy to develop lots of new contacts and relationships with people, no matter where they might be in the world; you can make contact with someone in Bermuda as easily as someone in Birmingham. As we'll see shortly, because of new web-based technology, the opportunities for networking are available to each and every one of us.

There's a great example I'd like to use here on the power of networking...

Do you remember a story a few years back about a young guy from Wiltshire, Alex Tew, who needed to raise money to pay for his University Education? He came up with the idea of **The Million Dollar Homepage.** The idea was simple, a homepage consisting of a million pixels arranged in a 1000 x 1000 grid, the image based links on it were sold for a $1 per pixel in 10 x 10 blocks. The aim of the site was to sell all of the pixels in the image, generating a million dollars for the website owner. It took about 5 months to sell all of the images and grossed $1,037,100 in income.

How did he do it?

- ✓ He was creative, wasn't afraid to be different and...
- ✓ ***Networking***

He rubbed shoulders, online with influential people, started to get noticed, an early form of viral marketing, and in the space of 5 months ended up on the BBC breakfast TV programme. In a nutshell, he had fun, was creative and he went for it. And the end result? Over a million dollars in income from one idea and he got a profile that has set him up as an online entrepreneur.

This example is more one of how networking can be very useful for promoting yourself and your business than how to land your dream job. Nevertheless, it hopefully shows you just how powerful networking can be.

Are you *still* really thinking that you're better off following the traditional route of sitting behind your computer, day-in, day-out, filling in job applications and emailing them to recruitment agencies and companies?

Networking Through Social Media (LinkedIn and Twitter)

Technology is advancing at a rate that sometimes seems almost impossible to keep up with. This is having an enormous impact upon the job markets as well as how we work. As a result of technology, an individual can now work for a company in New York from her home in Nottingham. Five years ago, Facebook barely existed; Twitter didn't exist at all. What will the world look like 10 years from now? Your guess is as good as mine, but I know it will be different. I also know that we'll need to keep up and change with this rapidly advancing technology.

Social Media—in a few years we won't be calling it 'Social Media' (remember the 'Information Super Highway?')—has changed the internet from a place where we merely exchanged information to a place that puts people in touch with each other. You can make a connection today with someone you don't know, you can find out a lot of information about them, and they can find out a lot of information about you.

One upshot of these technological advancements is that networking is no longer about who your Dad knows, what school you went to, or who your next door neighbour happens to know. You can develop relationships with people *directly* by using social media.

There are a lot of social networking sites on the

internet, certainly far too many to cover here. The two I'm going to be focussing on are LinkedIn and Twitter. I'll be giving you a general introduction to these social media in this section, and showing you how you can use them to find opportunities in the next section.

Before we move on, though, now would be a good time to briefly look at what employers are looking for in a potential candidate, this will help you to see just why using social media is so powerful in helping you to land your dream job.

The 3 elements that hiring managers want;

You should remember that you will not stand a chance of landing a great job in IT unless you can ***prove yourself***. In other words, you need to be able to demonstrate that you can *do* the job, and that you can do it *well*.

But there are two other things that hiring managers want to know before they offer you a job:

1. Will you *enjoy* the job?
2. Will they enjoy working with *you*?

You can give evidence of all of these things—ability; passion for the job; easy to get on with—by using social media.

Do you see how?

You can prove you can do the job. Okay, you might not have worked commercially in a specific area but you can build a reputation, online, that proves you know what you're talking about.

You can show your passion for your speciality by writing

a blog about it, making some 'how to' videos on YouTube, or answering questions in groups on LinkedIn.

Twitter is open. You can make friends with people who work in the jobs you want to work in. Over time, you can build relationships and trust. These people will then want to work with you.

Also, remember that the vast majority of jobs are not advertised; they go to people that employers know. Social media allows you to be that person. Using social networking media allows you to tap into what's called the 'hidden' job market, the jobs that aren't advertised.

Open the door to the hidden job market which shows you how to identify real time job opportunities by accessing my online video course covers see back of book for more details on how you can gain *instant access* to this little known information. Or simply visit www.brightstarttraining.com/itpro

Hopefully, you'll now be able to see why the use of social networks is so powerful for helping you to land your dream job. As I promised earlier, we'll now move on to look at the two most important social networking sites for finding that perfect job.

An Introduction to LinkedIn and Twitter

The vast majority of us use 'social media' or 'social networking sites'. Most of you reading this will be using Facebook, probably Twitter, and no doubt lots of other sites. I'm going to assume that you know what social media is, and I'm also going to assume that you use it and have a basic knowledge of it. This book isn't a guide to social media, it's an introduction to how you can use the power of social media to help you to find a great job. The two sites that are going to be the most helpful for you are LinkedIn and Twitter.

LinkedIn.

LinkedIn is **THE** network for business. The vast majority of experienced IT professionals, Hiring Managers, and Recruiters are already on LinkedIn. Quite simply: if you're not on LinkedIn, you need to be. It gives you huge amounts of information on companies, as well as the people who work at those companies, the jobs they do, and the skills they have.

Entire books have been written about LinkedIn, so I don't need to waste space by going into great detail (also, I go into much more detail about LinkedIn in the next section); but let's look at some of the most important parts of your profile that you need to complete.

The top 10 tips for your LinkedIn Profile:

1. Complete your profile to **100%.** You most definitely need to include a photo (and not the one where you're dressed as a clown at someone's party drinking Vodka). Also, think carefully about your headline; this is the first thing that people will see. ***Remember:*** First impressions count, on line as much as in person.
2. Use the Summary Section to show what you can

do for a future employer and why you would be a great new member of their team.

3. Specialities should include keywords; the areas where you have skills, as many of them as you can think of.

4. Website links. If you have a blog, or a website, link to it but make sure the site is something that you want a potential employer to see. Professionalism is *key* here.

5. Link in your Twitter account; this way, your connections can become followers (and vice versa).

6. Update your status regularly; comment on other peoples' comments; join in the conversation. 'Add value' to other people.

7. Join groups that are relevant to the area you want to work in and become an active member of the group. 'Make friends'.

8. Offer to help solve other people's problems *without* expecting anything in return.

9. If someone gets in touch with you, respond; use any communication to build results.

10. Search for companies who employ the sorts of jobs you want and follow them; find out who works there and, over time, look to network with

> them. *But remember*: networking is about them not you, so be friendly, offer help, and get to know them, don't just ask for a job.

Some people assume that LinkedIn is just an online CV or a directory. It is both of these things, but it is also a lot more. LinkedIn will work for you. It is **THE** place to network online, and it is a tool that you need to get very good at using ***now***, start on it today.

Twitter.

The other social networking site I want to talk about here is Twitter. Again, books have been written about Twitter so I'm not going to go into any great detail here. I'm not a Twitter expert but I do know that Twitter is one of the most powerful web-based social networks and, along with LinkedIn, the one you *have* to use.

Why is Twitter so important?

Twitter is completely open, you can make contact with anyone. And, if you're engaging enough, they may well respond. How many CVs or calls would you have to make to the CEO of a big company to get your message in front of her or him? It doesn't matter how many, you wouldn't, however with Twitter you *can*.

The CEO example above is perhaps a little extreme but, hopefully, it gives you the idea that on Twitter you can follow and communicate with real people in real time who can help you. The trick, though, is to be friendly. Comment on tweets and join conversations. Imagine that you're making friends face-to-face and behave in the same way. Again, ***don't fall into the trap of just asking for a job***, this will never work.

In an earlier section, I gave an example of a particular job where over a thousand people applied by sending me their CVs via email. Not one made contact via Twitter; yet, this is the area that's most likely to get my attention, as much as anything because it's different (for now at least).

Using Twitter can help you to do that all important thing of *differentiating yourself.*

As well as being open and instant, Twitter has another unique feature, it allows you to tap into 'public consciousness'. This means that it enables you to get ideas, help, and feedback. A tweet to your network can be re-tweeted; your message can be seen by thousands—even hundreds of thousands—of people. It's a great way to start building relationships.

If you're not on LinkedIn, you need to be. Exactly the same goes for Twitter.

Twitter is a little less formal than LinkedIn. You might also notice that the profile on LinkedIn takes some work; trust me, it is worth it. The opposite is true for Twitter, it's very simple.

How to get started on Twitter;

The first two things you need to do are to pick a username and write your 'bio'. Your bio—short for 'biography'—is a short description of you and appears on your profile.

Username.

As you're going to be using your Twitter profile as part of

your job search, I'd recommend that, for your username, you use either your name (or a variation off) or something reasonably professional that you'd be happy for future employers to see.

And, as with all Social Media, a good photo is important.

Bio.

As Twitter is a bit less formal that LinkedIn, the bio is where you can show a bit of your personality. The way I'd write it is like this: Think of it as if you were answering the question "*can you tell me a bit about yourself?*"

For example, my bio is:

"I get jobs for people and people for jobs. I try hard to be nice, open, honest, deliver what I promise, and make friends. Founder, Remit Resources IT Recruitment."

Once you're set up on Twitter, how successful you are will depend upon how you use it. (This applies to all of the tools we mention).

My 6 top tips for 'Twitter':

1. Follow industry blogs and news sites;
2. Join in on conversations; bring something different and new to the conversation;
3. Be yourself, have fun, and be respectful;
4. Ask intelligent questions that add to, or even start, conversations;
5. Post original tweets. In other words, don't just re-tweet others, join in with your own thoughts;

6. Include a professional photograph and bio.

Things to avoid on 'Twitter':

- × Don't talk only about yourself
- × Don't just ask for a job
- × Don't pick fights with people
- × Don't whinge or moan
- × Don't be afraid to share your opinion
- × Don't use a silly Twitter name
- × Absolutely do not spam
- × Dnt txt spk..... !
- × Do not tweet too much (5 or 6 tweets a day is about right, maybe more if you're following a particular event or something of interest)
- × Finally, do *not* tweet if you've been drinking. Alcohol makes us lose our inhibitions and to say things that, the next day, we might deeply regret.

Summary

In this section we've looked at how and why it's so important to network if you're trying to land your ideal job. Since almost all of us now have access to the internet, networking has never been easier and the number of contacts you can develop is potentially limitless.

The top 2 sites that will be the most helpful to you in terms of your career are:-

1. **LinkedIn**
2. **Twitter**

As an IT graduate, you should find it easy to set yourself up on both of these sites. Once you've published your bio, you'll be able to use these sites to take advantage of the many opportunities they give you for landing a great job. What are these opportunities and how do you go about grasping them? We'll find out in the next section.

New to LinkedIn? ***Get ahead now***, and find out exactly how to set up LinkedIn and Twitter, as well as tweetdeck with real time training. If you're smart, LinkedIn should become your go to site for building relationships and getting connected to the right people who in turn can help you get the IT job of your dreams. Visit www.brightstarttraining.com/itpro now for full access.

Using Social Media to Find Real Time Opportunities

In the last section, I introduced you to two of the most important—probably THE most important—social networking sites: **LinkedIn and Twitter**. In this section, I'm going to show you how you can use these social media to find real time opportunities for a great career in IT

We'll start with **LinkedIn**; why you should join LinkedIn and how can you use it to turbo-charge your job search.

LinkedIn

You'll remember from the last section that LinkedIn is **THE** network for business. (And if you've got access to the online training course, your profile will already be working for you!) The vast majority of experienced IT Professionals, Hiring Managers, and Recruiters are already on LinkedIn. LinkedIn is Facebook for business, although it's different to Facebook in that the etiquette for using it is different. LinkedIn is professional; it is NOT a place for sharing your stories about the weekend, latest holidays, or how drunk you were last night. LinkedIn is where you find professionals, and these professionals may one day be able to help you to get a great job in IT.

LinkedIn is so helpful for finding real time job opportunities because it allows you to use it cleverly to have access to the right people, access to people that, just a few years ago, you wouldn't have stood a chance of getting access to. It's also a huge database, you can see people who work at almost any company in the world, all over the world; you can get a feel for the skill sets in these different companies and what types of people they hire.

The other key aspect of LinkedIn is that it's a tool to enable you to have two way communication with people. So, it's both a database and a communication tool.

The main difference between the vast majority of IT professionals and the vast majority of people looking to work in IT is that the people who are looking to work in IT aren't on LinkedIn. ***You really must be on LinkedIn!*** We'll talk in lots of detail throughout this section about LinkedIn and how to use it to grasp real time job opportunities.

How to use LinkedIn to get a great job;

At the start of this section, I mentioned that the etiquette for using LinkedIn properly is different to Facebook. How? The main way is that you must ***give value*** first without expecting anything in return. In other words, blindly approaching people saying, *"Give me a job"* is a big fat no-no! You will NOT get a job this way, for a start, you will sound way too desperate. Instead, use this medium to *build relationships* by entering into two-way dialogue with people; give your potential employers (or people connected to potential employers) a reason to help you, what's in it for them? Remember from the last section that networking is about *them*, not you, so be friendly, offer help, and get to know them. All of these things are extremely important. As an example, why not join a group for professionals in the area you're looking to specialise in?

What sorts of things are the people in the group talking about? Can you help out by posting a link to a relevant blog post you've seen?

Get your profile right;

How do you get your profile right? Throughout this book I've spoken a lot about how important it is for you to be creative and different, these are the two key things that you need to bear in mind for everything you do. Be a little bit creative; think a little bit. I'm not saying behave like Jack Nicolson in *The Shining* (!)—don't be a crazy, weird, totally off-the-wall person—but *do* be a little bit different in how you approach things and what you expect, and do things *differently* to the average LinkedIn user.

Your profile picture:

First things first: A professional photo is paramount; statistics show that your profile is five times more likely to be visited if you have one. The photo needs to be a clear shot of your face and it needs to be a professional photo, pretty obvious. We don't want pictures of your dog, cat, favourite pop star, or favourite football team. We want to see a picture of *you*, and it needs to be a *professional* picture of you.

A professional photograph doesn't mean you have to look miserable, quite the opposite. It's a well-known fact that smiling makes us more attractive. People will therefore warm to you more, and will be more likely to approach you, if you're smiling in your profile photograph. At the same time, be careful not to go overboard, you don't want to look like Wallace from Wallace and Gromit or

Penguin from Batman. Your photo will give people their first impression of you and, as we'll see later on, first impressions are extremely important in helping you to land your dream job.

You're looking for a job so remember this when you're setting up your profile, let people know that you're in the job market.

For LinkedIn secrets to success - follow my online training course on how to set up your profile to gain maximum searches and get your online profile seen by the people that matter, simply visit www.brightstarttraining.com/itpro

Header line:

One of the first things you'll notice when you're using your profile is a *header line*. You need to use this to be *creative* and to come up with something different. (Don't put on there that you're unemployed.) Why don't you go and have a look at my profile for a moment which is at http://www.linkedin.com/in/remitresources. What does my profile say? Does it say I'm a recruiter, like hundreds—if not thousands—of other recruiters on LinkedIn? No. I have a unique header line: *Chief Executive Talent Spotter*. Now, what does that mean? Exactly the same as 'Recruitment Specialist' or 'Owner of a Recruitment Business'. But it has an entirely different, and far more interesting ring to it. It grabs people's attention and they comment on it. How many other people on LinkedIn have that as their job title? None.

So, be a bit different. Also, make it a little bigger than you are. If you're great, *tell* people why you're great. Say what you can do for them, and what you can do technically. Remember that you're a valuable person with a lot to offer so don't be afraid to 'blow your own trumpet'.

Who uses LinkedIn?

The greatest beneficiaries of LinkedIn are recruiters. It wasn't designed as such, but that's what it has turned into. After recruiters, the other major users are salespeople, and there are people on there who are just looking to network. But the biggest users of LinkedIn are recruiters, which is great news for you as a job seeker. So, when you're setting up your profile, make it look different, make it crisp, and make it look good. Also, make sure it's readable. It needs to be like a brochure or your website—high quality—and it needs to sell what you can do, just as your CV needs to sell, it is an advert for yourself.

People use LinkedIn to search for particular skill sets. If you don't have any great experience, what should you do? Under the 'Experience' section, simply state how you can add value. Why would you be a great person to hire? For example, you might want to include a link to a web page you've developed, or those YouTube videos we mentioned earlier, or mention the virtual network you've built. Include something that *proves* you have experience (even if it isn't commercial).

Of course, since you're looking for a job, you'll also need to make sure that you're contactable so put your Twitter name and email address on your LinkedIn profile. If you don't want to give your main e-mail address then create one specifically for LinkedIn. (While we're on the topic of email addresses, bear in mind that your email address needs to sound professional. Being professional means being a little more serious, and fluffybunny@hopmail.com doesn't look very professional to say the least).

The idea is that you need to provide enough contact information to enable a recruiter or hiring manager to get in touch with you easily. Put a link on your profile to your blog (if you don't have a blog, you should have, the investment in time is worth it, but make the blog something that shows your knowledge of, and passion for, IT). This is the area in your profile where you can prove what you can do. You might remember that earlier in the book we spoke about CVs and what the purpose of a CV is. That purpose is to prove you can do the job in order to get you an interview; this is precisely why you're using LinkedIn, to *prove* yourself professionally.

Remember that LinkedIn is a relational database. You therefore need to include keywords on your profile that relate to your area of expertise and your skill set. Include as many relevant keywords as you can think of, this will increase the chances of people finding you. If you decide to specialise in developing software, make sure the keywords, 'software developer' and 'software programmer' are included. Finally, make sure that all of the technologies you have experience in are included, for example, PHP, VBScript, or C#.

The main thing to remember from all of this is this: Get your profile *right*. Make it look professional and make it something that you're *proud* to show people.

LION

When you start using LinkedIn, you'll often see the acronym 'LION'. LION stands for *"LinkedIn Open Networker"* and is really useful if you want to make lots of connections. It basically means that you're not going to block people, say you don't know people, or say that you're being spammed if people are getting in touch with you. Most recruiters are LIONs because they want to connect with lots of people. It would be a good idea to make yourself a LION and advertise this on your profile because having lots of connections is really important (I explain why below).

How to use LinkedIn

We're going to start this section off with some tips on how to use LinkedIn quickly and easily. Once you have the hang of it, you'll probably find that LinkedIn will be your main 'go to' site when looking for a job.

When you first start using LinkedIn, you might find it a little daunting, you won't have any connections but you'll see that some people have thousands. But making connections will be so valuable to you because it will open up your network significantly, it allows you to see into almost every company on LinkedIn (which is every company in the world). Make it your goal to get more than five hundred connections. I know this sounds like an awful lot but you can actually soon be working towards this number if you start with LIONs. As I mentioned a moment ago, you know LIONs are going to accept your invite, so this is a great way of starting to quickly build up your connections.

Making Connections.

Don't try to connect with someone you don't know; the person you connected with could report you as 'spam' or a 'I don't know' and your account can potentially be blocked. Only send invites to connect with the people you already *know (if they are not an open networker).*

➲ **Remember:** you need to show how you can be of value to your potential connections

Your potential connections will be thinking, *"what's in it for me?"* so talk to people first (via email or the Answer and Group sections of LinkedIn), *then* invite them to connect with you. For example, you might be able to show your expertise in an area by answering a question really well. Demonstrating your knowledge in this way is extremely helpful because it enables you to *prove yourself;* so, when the time comes, that connection will recommend or refer you to someone who can give you a job. Think just how much more powerful this is going to be than if you're one of the couple of hundred people applying for something. Or, what if the job is never advertised and you hear it on the grape vine? This is where LinkedIn can *really* help you to get ahead.

Researchers have shown that people love being flattered, we like to hear how great we are. Salespeople often use flattery to persuade their customers, and you could try using this strategy yourself on LinkedIn. For example, leave comments on people's articles or blog posts; similarly, if you're speaking to a hiring manager, always follow up your conversation with a connection. You want to be connecting with everyone you talk to or email, explaining *why* you're wanting to connect; *but remember:* that explanation should never be *"I need a job"*.

In summary, give value to your potential connections in *advance* of connecting with them, and wait for the precise moment when they can help you. This moment *will* come but you may have to be patient, it might not be now; it might not be part of a current job search; but it *could* be something where they can help you in years to come. There will always come a time when your connections can help you, so, the more people you can connect with the better.

How great is this; you're using LinkedIn to make friends with people who might be able to help you *land your dream job*

Jobs section;

As the title suggests, the Jobs section is where you can search for jobs, and where companies who are recruiting will go to hire people for jobs. You can also get e-mail alerts for jobs so that you can be sure to not miss any opportunities, and can narrow down your search so that it only looks for jobs in a particular location.

Why is this better than joining a standard job forum?

The really great thing about the Jobs section on LinkedIn is that you can see people you know who either work at these companies or who you can refer to these companies. This is why it's so important to invest your time in joining groups and making friends with people on there. *Remember*: you need to show that you have some expertise; some knowledge. These people can have a direct impact on whether you can get a job. How? Well, when a Software Development Manager, Database Manager, or any recruitment manager is looking to hire someone, they're going to talk to their colleagues and friends. If these people know someone, they're going to recommend that person. The job will not be advertised. If you've built up a relationship with that Manager, you will stand a much better chance of getting the job.

These things take time though, they don't happen overnight. Nevertheless, if you've just started chatting to someone and you notice that one of their own connections is looking to hire, you still stand a chance of being recommended, *provided* you have shown that you're likeable and have some knowledge in the area specific to the job. Can you see why LinkedIn is so much more powerful than other job boards? It allows you to see people, engage in two-way communication with them, and develop relationships with them.

Companies:

As the name suggests, the 'Companies' tab in LinkedIn allows you to search for companies. Not only does it enable you to search for companies in your area, it also allows you to search for companies of a particular size and companies in a particular industry or sector. To use the example of software development again, you can use the companies tab to look for companies that specifically hire developers. So, you can see exactly what type of people different companies employ. It's a great source of leads.

There are two advantages to being able to see the types of people that a particular company employs: Firstly, when you're thinking about how you should present yourself to them, you know exactly what they're looking for, clearly, this is going to be extremely helpful in terms of giving you information about which aspect or aspects of your skill set to focus upon; the second great thing is that, once you've looked at a particular company, you can follow it and get lots of information about it, when someone leaves, you'll find out; when someone gets promoted, you'll find out. And you can find these things out quickly because you can arrange to receive email updates when changes like this happen. You'll find out immediately when someone has moved from a particular job in a company, it's all in real-time. It does rely on people updating their profiles, but people generally do update their profiles when they move on. When someone does move on, grasp the opportunity to expand your network, connect with someone at that company. It seems daunting if you don't have many connections—I understand that—but we all have to start somewhere. Just start looking at it.

News tab;

The next tab to look at in LinkedIn is the News tab. I talk in more detail about the relevance of news when you're preparing for interviews in step 3; how important it is to be jenned up on the latest developments in a company that you wish to work for so that your interviewer knows that you have your 'finger on the pulse' and that you're interested in what the company does. The news tab on LinkedIn is an excellent way of keeping up-to-date with company news, you'll find out so much information about what's going on in companies. And finding out just what's going on within a company is helpful not only for your interview, it gives you something to talk about when you're reaching out to connect with someone who works there. Researching the latest developments within companies is far more valuable than blindly sending out CV after CV, not to mention far more interesting. Invest time in learning about the companies you're interested in.

Answers:

The Answer section in LinkedIn is where you can *really* start to give yourself some exposure. As I've mentioned in previous sections, one of the difficulties you're likely to face is the 'no commercial experience' problem. The 'answers' section of LinkedIn helps you to surmount this problem.

How?

By joining in on conversations and answering questions about the specific areas you're interested in. In other words, you can use the answers section to *prove* that you have some expertise. You can start conversations on there, make friends, and help people, all of these are great ways to develop professional relationships.

Try to set yourself the goal of answering at least ONE question every day in this section. It will soon become a habit. It takes a bit of time, yes, but if you're serious about landing a great job this will be a very wise investment of your time.

Blogging platform;

One of the ways in which you can prove your expertise and get a little bit of following is by blogging. If you've ever had a blog, you'll probably know how difficult it can be to get traffic to it. But not with LinkedIn. LinkedIn has a WordPress plug-in which automatically allows your blog to be seen on your profile. So, if people are searching for you and if you're connecting with them, they'll see your blog.

Blogging on LinkedIn is a great way to *get noticed.*

Groups:

Groups are one of the most important areas of LinkedIn so I'm quite surprised that it's not as widely used as it should be. You can join up to fifty groups, and I strongly recommend that you use all of those fifty groups. To get you started, go to my own group at www.brightstarttraining.com/linkedingroup and join the conversation. You'll get a warm welcome, I promise, and I'll answer every comment on there. Let's make friends and get to know each other better.

You might be wondering about what sorts of groups to join. There are two main group types that you need to join on LinkedIn if you want a great job in IT: You obviously need to join groups for job seekers, but you should also join groups that are technical where you can start to build relationships with experienced people in the area that you want to work in. You'll be able to learn from these people, and might be able to offer them a little bit of help; you'll find out what's relevant to them, what's important in their business sector, and what the latest technologies are; you'll find out what challenges they're currently facing and a whole host of other valuable information. Join as many of these groups as you can.

When you join a group, join in, don't be a 'lurker' (this is a technical term that's used to describe social networkers who merely observe what's happening on social media sites). By all means, observe to start with—you'll want to get a feel for the tone of the group—but don't be afraid to join in on the conversation. Introduce yourself, explain why you're there, and join the conversation in a professional yet friendly manner. Don't forget: you need to *add value*.

And remember:

- *Don't* make the conversation all about you,
- *Don't* hassle people for jobs, and
- *Don't* spam people.

These are not great ways to win friends and influence people.

What other advantages do Groups give you? Once you're a member of a group you can message other members of the same group directly and you can search for them at LinkedIn. This is very powerful because LinkedIn works on connections and degrees of connections, the bigger your network, the more people and the more companies you can see. So, with LinkedIn, the bigger your network is, the better it is.

But beware, it's not like Twitter. You can't just blindly connect with everyone because people will block you. Joining groups on LinkedIn helps you to get around this problem, you can message other group members and explain to them what your situation is. You can also send them a little personal note explaining your situation and asking if they'd like to connect with you. You'd be amazed at the response to this.

When you're inviting a member of a particular group to connect with you, make it personal. For example, don't write, "Dear Sir,"; instead say, "Hi, Richard." Explain that you want to break into the sector (as opposed to directly asking for a job), that you're hoping to learn from them, and whether they'd be happy to connect with you. People *do* respond to this approach, and if you send out 1000 messages hundreds will respond.

Let's look at an example...

"Hi Richard, my name's John. We share the C# Developer's Group. I'm looking to connect with a couple of key players in this sector as, eventually, it's an area I want to work in. Would you be happy to connect with me?"

Simple, isn't it? It's very effective too, I've seen this approach work so many times. If you use this approach you can't get blocked; it's unobtrusive so nobody minds. The worst a person can do is not respond, but you can start to make some new contacts. In general, people like to help; so, as long as you use a friendly approach like the one in the above example, people will want to help.

When you're looking at LinkedIn to search, it limits the search results to three degrees of connection (for example, if you know the person directly, then it's a 1st level connection; if you know someone through someone in your 1st level connections, then it's a 2nd level connection). It also limits search results to a certain number. That number will depend upon what plan you have (in other words, what you pay for) with LinkedIn, your limit could be one hundred results, three hundred, or five hundred, depending upon what's included in your plan.

Which plan is best?

At this stage—you're only just getting started on LinkedIn—the free plan is fine for you.

However, if you want to turbo-boost your LinkedIn potential—I'm sure you will once you get the hang of the basics—and discover a really powerful way to search more than 500 results, then simply visit www.brightstarttraining.com/itpro

Skills;

'Skills' is a new feature in LinkedIn. It's in Beta at the moment but it's very, very useful. Have a look at it now. Type in a technology or a skill and it will give you the definition of it. It will also show you related skills, professionals with skills in that area, companies that employ that type of person, demand for that skill, and groups of people with that skill set. It's incredibly powerful.

Hopefully, you can now see just what an incredibly powerful tool LinkedIn is for getting access to real-time job opportunities. You really need to use it and take advantage of the powerful potential it can offer you. Let's now see how you can use Twitter to do precisely the same...

Twitter

Twitter is a social network, but it's also a lot more. It's a communication tool and, because it's open, it's more powerful than most other social media. By 'open' I mean that you can follow and interact with anyone, and anyone on twitter can follow and interact with you. That is very powerful. LinkedIn and Facebook rely on invitations and knowing people in advance, but this is not the case with Twitter, you can connect with anyone. The only thing that stops you having a relationship with someone on Twitter is how interesting you are and how relevant you are to their conversation.

Twitter is less formal than LinkedIn and more interactive. It's also very, very easy to use. This ease of use is a good thing in some ways, but a bad thing in others. On the good side, it's very easy to establish relationships with people, in the recruitment business, I've found and placed a lot of people from Twitter recently. On the potentially negative side, you need to bear in mind that everything you say or do is visible, and all of this combines to form your *online reputation*. So, it can be very damaging if you tweet things that are unprofessional or are otherwise bad. There have been a few stories in the press recently about people who have tweeted things that they shouldn't have and regretted it. So, be careful and aware of what you say on Twitter, everything you say and do is part of your online reputation.

"Hang on a minute", I hear you say, *"what does he mean by online reputation?"*

Why your online reputation is critical;

Your online reputation is no different to your offline reputation. So, it's extremely important. Each time you form a professional relationship with someone, the first thing they'll do is go to Google and check you out. Whenever you go for a job, the very first thing the vast majority of potential employers will do is go on line and find out about you. Once they're there, what they see is the impression they'll form of you. They will make decisions based on what they see of you online.

In Step 3, I speak about preparing for interviews using LinkedIn to see what organisations do and the types of people who work there. But don't think that people aren't going to do the same to you, they are. Every single thing that's out there on the World Wide Web about you contributes to your reputation and who you are. This might not be fair but this is the real world (and, if you're honest, you'll admit to doing the same yourself). So, be aware that people will look at you and make their minds up about you from what they see of you on line.

This doesn't mean you have to boring; that you can't show your true personality or who you are. Your tweets don't have to be all about IT; they don't have to be only about work. They *can* give an insight into your personality. Take a minute or two to look at my twitter feed which is @ceotalentscout. You'll notice a few things about this. My profession is recruitment so I tweet job adverts. As an aside to this, I get responses to job adverts and get candidates that I place in jobs through twitter. I tweet blog articles that I've written on how to get jobs in IT, how to prepare for job interviews, and how to follow the latest trends that are happening; I tweet quick interview tips; I respond to people and talk to people on twitter. I join conversations on the things I'm interested in, whether they be about recruitment, preparing for interviews and how to get great jobs, or the latest developments in technology and the latest cool gadgets. I re-tweet interesting articles that my followers might be interested in.

But also—and you don't have to dig too far beneath the surface to discover this—I tweet a lot about football. And I tweet a lot about golf, rugby, and tennis. As you can probably tell, I'm an avid sports spectator, and while I'm watching a match I'll tweet about it; if I'm going anywhere interesting, or doing something different, then I'll tweet about it; I'll use foursquare to check into places and let people know what I'm doing. None of this has anything directly to do with being a recruiter. But it's good fun *and* it's a way of making friends and starting to interact with people. Also, when someone looks at my twitter feed—be they a new client and looking to hire me as a head hunter, or a new candidate looking to apply for a job with my firm—they can hopefully see that I'm a pretty rounded individual – I'm pretty professional with work but I'm also not shy of having a bit of fun; I've got different interests outside of work, and some of those interests might appeal to other people. They also build up an idea of who I am.

So, don't be afraid to show your true personality. *But remember:* if you're going to use Twitter as a professional tool, you need to have some professionalism in there.

Bio and username:

Your bio on twitter is important, it needs to say what you do but it also needs to be a little bit eye catching. It needs to make someone look at you and want to follow you. Mine is the same as my LinkedIn bio: *"I get jobs for people, and people for jobs. I try hard to be nice, open, honest, deliver what I promise, and make friends. I'm the founder of Remit Resources, IT recruitment."* Now what does that say about me? I think it shows that I'm normal and down to earth; I think it gives you an idea of how I like to conduct myself and my business.

Have a look at what other recruiters put on their profile, you'll tend to find it's pretty boring stuff.

Don't be boring. You've only got your 140 characters for your bio, and you need to be 'searchable', so think very carefully about your bio and what it says about you.

You should also think very carefully about your **username**. This is on everything you tweet so pick something sensible. This is even more important when you're using Twitter to network and build up relationships with people who can have an influence on your future career. If you can get your name, then get it; however, it's not always easy to get your name, and if you can't get it then don't go for something crazy, something that makes you look like an oddball, or something that makes you look like a wild party animal.

You can still go for something a bit different, though, there's nothing wrong with that. Mine is @ceotalentscout. What does that mean? Well it means I scout for talent. I'm a recruiter, that's what I do. And my job title is 'CEO Talent Scout'. Different, huh? How many recruiters do you know with that title? So, do use something that can make you look different. Be creative but don't go crazy, it needs to be professional.

A further, very important, part of setting up your twitter profile is your **web address**. You can use this web address to link to anything—your blog or personal website, for example—but the one I would recommend is your *LinkedIn profile*. Linking your web address to your LinkedIn profile means that anyone who is looking at you has the opportunity to immediately go to your more in-depth professional profile. In effect, this helps you to create a big circle, someone might find you on Twitter, but they can then go and immediately see you on LinkedIn simply by clicking a link. But you don't want to send them off to your blog, send them off to your professional profile instead. They can then connect and see your professional profile as well.

How to use Twitter to find great jobs:

You can use twitter to find a job in two ways; both of these are important, but I think the first point will ultimately give you the longer term success. If you've already watched and implemented the online training course to get your twitter account up and running, you should already be identifying real time job opportunities.

1. Create relationships with people who can help you.

As I said earlier, Twitter is a completely open platform, there's nothing to stop you from communicating with some of the most famous and influential people in the world. BUT you need to be ***interesting.*** The popular, famous, celebrities on twitter will talk and re-tweet you ***IF*** you have interesting conversations. So, the only thing that stops you from connecting with people is how you interact with them.

You don't need to connect with famous people though, although you might impress your friend if you can say that you've been re-tweeted by Bill Gates, you don't need to connect with Bill Gates to get a job as a Microsoft Developer. What you *do* need to do, though, is connect with professional people in those areas you want to work in.

Elsewhere in the book I talk about specialising, especially as a software developer. So, you might use twitter to connect with other software developers. You can follow as many of them as you like. When you start following these developers you can find out what's important in their professional lives, what sorts of things they're talking about, and who they're talking to. What technology are they talking about? What problems do they have? What buzz words are they using? All of these things are key bits of information that I urge you to start using *today* to build a relationship.

You would never have been given the chance to do this in the old days, you would need to have been invited to a networking group. If you weren't part of the club it was difficult to break into that club. These days you don't need to do that, you can use Twitter to do it. Easy.

As well as checking out professionals, you can also use Twitter to check out companies that you want to work with, and the people who work in those companies. You can connect with bloggers who blog on the subjects you're addressing and the industry you work in.

➲ But remember the **fundamental rule**; *it's not all about you!*

Initially, you want to make friends; join in on the conversation. *Don't just ask for a job.* Add value first, the opportunities will come. Build up awareness amongst the peer group. Show who you are; you're a fun, bright, and intelligent person, and you're thoughtful. Show what you can offer through your daily interactions with these people. If you make a good impression then you'll move on from Twitter to phone, email, and eventually to meeting these people in person. At this point, you've gone beyond an online relationship and you're going somewhere to being friends. And people *want* to work with people they like.

Remember*: the vast majority of jobs are never advertised, *they come from recommendations.

And, as I hinted at a second ago, it's not about the old school ties these days; it's not about who your Dad knows. The rules that were there in the past that prevented people from joining clubs aren't there anymore, because you can use Twitter.

2. Use Twitter as a real-time job board.

You can also use Twitter as a real time job board. As I've said elsewhere in the book, you're not at the right stage in your career to use recruiters; instead, hunt out jobs via companies that are hiring directly. Look for professionals who are already in the industry talking about roles in their companies and so on. The beauty of Twitter is that it's in real time, it gives you the advantage of being the first to hear about a job.

Search engines:

Twitter has job search engines. There are lots of them but, for now, try www.twitjobsearch.com. This site lets you enter technical terms. If you add a location you'll see that it then brings up the results of those jobs on Twitter. This is really powerful, great, stuff. We're going to be talking about finding jobs and setting up searches in the next section.

Twitter management software;

You'll notice that the more you use Twitter, the more people follow you and the more people you follow. And the more searches you have running in there, the more important it is to organise this data, otherwise it will become unmanageable very quickly. There are a number of tools—called *twitter management software*—available to help you with this. The two I use are *Hootsuite* and *Tweetdeck*.

Hootsuite and Tweetdeck.

Hootsuite is free (to a certain extent) and there is a subscribable version; *Tweetdeck* is completely free. They're both good. Go and get yourself an account and set it up. When you set up the software you'll realise you can group things in columns so you can set up searches. So, go in there and set up keyword searches around the technologies you want to work in. For example, if you want to work in C#, or SQL or Cloud computing—whatever area you want to work in—go on there and set up some searches. The search will throw up loads of information around the area you want to work in: It will show you the professionals who are talking about those technologies, bloggers who are commenting on them, and all of the new news. This is a very powerful tool because the more information you know about an industry or business sector, the better.

Also, include speech marks around terms like "we're recruiting", "we're hiring", "my company need...", "send me your CV", and "anyone know a developer". What other things might people be saying along these lines? Run some searches of your own. Experiment a little bit and set up some searches in real time when this information is being broadcasted on Twitter.

Hashtags:

Hashtags identify specific conversations in Twitter. So, again in your Twitter management software, set up a column for #jobs, #careers, #hiring, #interview, and #jobsearch (you can set up dozens and dozens and dozens of them). Explore and find the ones that are relevant to you, and set them up. It will show you who you should be following in companies that you want to work in. Once you've got that information you can answer some of the questions. Add a bit of value. Don't spam them; don't stalk them. But do help them, offer a solution; point people in the right direction; engage with them and make friends with them. Follow Twitter feeds for the blogs that are relevant to technology, mashable, technorati, people who are in our industry and who are commenting on our industry. The information you can get here is really, really, powerful and it gives you a real time advantage to help you find the conversations that are interesting and that you can join in on.

The 4 golden rules of Twitter:

Rule # 1: You don't have to be clever or smart, but try and bring something new to the conversations that you join. So, add something to the conversation. It sounds like a bit of a cliché, but *add value*. Add value to the conversations in advance *without* expecting anything in return.

Rule # 2: Listen to the discussions, and don't always feel you have to comment on every discussion on everyone and everything. Sometimes, there's nothing wrong with listening, only joining in when you have something to add to the conversation.

Rule # 3: Don't be afraid to let your personality shine through. Think about it in terms of what it's like when you're making friends with someone in the real world (sometimes with these online things, it *is* the real world). Think about how you make friends with people face to face. And bear in mind you don't want to necessarily be writing about how you were drunk until four o'clock in the morning which is why you haven't prepared for your interview. If you put that type of tweet on there, someone will see it who you do not want to see it.

Rule # 4: Ask *intelligent* questions. Let your questions contribute to the conversation; make sure they are questions that add to the conversation and take it forward.

The questions you ask should make the people involved in the discussion *think* about things.

Bonus Rule #5: Don't just re-tweet. Draw on your own experiences and come up with original ideas. Start conversations, start discussions, and move things forward. Be original. *And remember:* If you walked into the reception of a company and started shouting at people to give you a job, the only guaranteed reaction you would get is a big fat *"no"*. It's just the same with Twitter.

Use Twitter to build relationships, give value in advance, and make friends - *you'll be amazed at the results.*

What do I mean by 'give value'?

I've spoken quite a bit about 'adding value' in this book and I think that now would be a good time to go into a little more detail about this. What does this mean? I've spotted three types of people on Twitter who don't add value. Firstly, there's the over-eager job seeker who only ever talks about himself. He continually makes the same point, sends out the same tweet, and continually says, *"Yes I can do this job, I can do this job, I can do this job"* without joining in on any conversations or listening because that's boring. These people never say anything interesting or relevant. They tweet about nonsense, the weather, and what they're having for lunch. We all know them.... if you're new to Twitter, you'll soon find them.

The second type of person who doesn't add value on twitter is the person who *never joins in*. They never say anything; never join in on any conversation, they're just too quiet.

And then there's the final type of person who we hear about on the news, the 'troll'. Trolls have nothing 'positive' to say about anyone. They want to fight, don't want to listen, and seem intent on saying negative things about people.

Do yourself a favour - don't be one of these types of people!

Twitter may seem daunting to start with, but it's great fun. And it will open up so many opportunities for you. People are finding jobs on Twitter every day. I hire people in my recruitment firm from Twitter. I've hired people who provide services to me from twitter; I've made friends with them on Twitter; I've got to know them on Twitter, and I've spent money with them. Whatever and whoever they may be— trainers, PA's, web designers, book keepers—I have made friends with these people and have hired them through Twitter. When I meet them for the first time, it feels like I already know them. This is all down to the power of Twitter.

Summary

To put all of this in a nutshell, **LinkedIn and Twitter** are *THE social networking sites* for finding real time opportunities in IT If you're not on both of these sites you *need* to be. Join up today, it's easy. Simply follow the advice I've outlined in this section and implement my guidelines (including the things to avoid).

Also, remember to:-

- ✓ Add value
- ✓ Show your personality, and
- ✓ Be willing to 'give before you receive'

By doing the three things above, you will differentiate yourself from the crowd, and you will show your passion and expertise (especially if you follow the third rule). Remember that it's critical to get a good 'online reputation' as this will assist you greatly in getting your ideal job.

STEP 3: Go Further

The New Rules of Job Hunting

The economy is slow. But the real reason that many people are struggling to find that perfect job isn't the slow economy. It's the fact that the world is changing. The way technology is being used in business is changing everything and we're only at the very start of that change.

You can't afford to wait for things to get better. When the economy gets better—and it will—this isn't going to automatically mean there will be a huge surplus of jobs. The competition will still be fierce and your approach will have to change.

In the future we will all be service providers. The successful ones amongst us will need to have specialist skills, and we will have to take responsibility for our own careers, no one else will do it for us.

The 3 new rules of job hunting:

➲ **New Rule #1: Be creative and be different.**

Find something that fits your personality and do it. There are lots of examples here www.brightstarttraining.com/itentrylevel. These show examples of what others, who have been in your situation, have done to be different. I'm not suggesting you do this; I'm saying you need to be creative. Don't be afraid to try something different, and find the approach that works for you.

➲ **New Rule #2: Your CV must sell!**

This is more the case now than ever because CVs are no longer the most important thing in getting a job (as we've seen, it's more important to specialise in a specific area; it's critical to use technology and social media to show what you can do; and it's even more important to build a network of contacts who can help you, and who you can help, initially expecting nothing in return).

➲ **New Rule #3: What does your personal brand say about you?**

What personal brand? Exactly! Do you have a personal website? If not, why not? It doesn't cost much and can be another way of 'building your brand' online. It can say who you are, what you do, and what you stand for. Employers and recruiters will Google you. When they do, what will they find? Make sure it's something positive, and something that shows your skills and your specialisms.

It's tough out there, but stay positive. This is easier said than done when you're facing rejection. You must stay positive, though, because your attitude is projected in everything you do. Read positive books, speak to positive people, and believe in yourself. Remember that positive things happen to positive people.

Get Interviews Easily

So far we've talked a lot about differentiating yourself

through specialising, and using social media to build contacts. We'll shortly be going on to talk in depth about preparing for interviews. Firstly, though, let's look at a couple of things that will make it easy for you to get interviews, the first is being aware of the 60 second rule, and the second is personalising your cover letters.

The 60 second rule:

Sixty seconds is how much time you have to make a first impression. Not long, is it? It's that first impression on which future employers will judge you, and it includes everything from what your social media sites say about you, and what impression your blog leaves, to your CV, covering letter, first call or interview with an employer...and everything in between.

This first 60 seconds makes a big difference. This is the time it takes for someone to make their mind up and make an initial assessment of you (often subconsciously, but they do it nevertheless).

Is this fair?

Probably not, but if you think about it, we do it all the time: If you go shopping, what do you buy? The thing that grabs your attention; the thing that stands out? If you see a top that doesn't look or feel right, how often do you go back to the shop to buy it later? It's the same when we meet people. We get gut feelings, make immediate decisions, and often find that those first impressions were right (or at least we think they're right as we've already made the decision).

Now you know that the first 60 seconds are crucial, you can give yourself a real *competitive advantage.*

We spoke earlier about the power of using social networking sites. The 60 second rule here dictates that you should make sure that your profiles stand out, that they're different, and that they capture the attention immediately. A potential employer will not hang around on your profile for very long unless it is attention-grabbing—they'll leave your page after just 60 seconds.

Some top tips for making a great first impression;

"Tell me about yourself...."

When you first speak to a prospective employer, the first question they will ask will be *"tell me about yourself?"* As I mentioned earlier when I was talking about preparing your Twitter bio, this is an answer you need to have ready. In order to be effective, it needs to be well thought-through, well prepared, and highly polished.

Tailor your cover letter.

Tailor a cover letter for each application you send. We've already talked about how much competition there is for every job, employers and recruiters will receive hundreds (often more) CVs every week. This is your opportunity to stand out; to shine. Use the cover letter as a chance to highlight relevant experience and how this relates to the job. The cover letter will be the first piece of documentation that your potential employer sees, so work hard on making the right first impression. (I go into more detail on cover letters in the next section.)

Follow up.

It's also important to follow up your application in a telephone call. But be relevant, concise, and engaging. So, instead of calling with the usual opening line of *"I just wanted to call to see if you had received my CV"*, or *"is the job still available?"*, have a few sentences prepared about how your experience relates directly to the job specified in the advert (just as you would in your cover letter). And don't call 10 times a day, you don't want to look like a stalker.

Have your answers ready...

Once you've grabbed the recruiter's attention, and you've shown him or her that you have the skills for the job, it isn't difficult to work out what the first couple of questions are going to be. Have the answers ready. Think about what you're going to say in advance and practice, it's not easy to give good spontaneous answers when the pressure is on.

It is key here to present the important information about you to a potential employer in a straightforward and engaging way. These tips are pretty simple—they're simple on purpose—but the sad fact is that most people do not make the extra effort; if you do, it will give you a real advantage.

Personalised cover letters;

I want to talk about cover letters for a while because so many people don't seem to be aware of what the purpose of a cover letter is. The purpose of the cover letter is to convince your potential employer why you are the right person for the job. In the last section, I mentioned how important it is to write a personalised cover letter for every job. Be honest with yourself for a moment: Do you? And, by personalised, I don't mean just changing the name and job title at the top; I mean actually taking the time to write something that clearly and concisely shows why you are the right person for that particular job.

So, your cover letter should be customised specifically to the requirements of each and every job. My experience tells me that hardly anyone ever does this. It's not unusual for me to advertise a job to which I get hundreds of responses, not one of which tells me—in straightforward, normal, language—why they're great for this job. So, again, if you can do this, you will stand out from the rest.

Let's look at a real example...

> Over the last few weeks, I've been advertising for an IT Manager for a small Microsoft Gold Partner based in South London. For the right person, it's a great opportunity: £45,000 salary, new technologies, plenty of project work, and the opportunity for progression.
>
> The company has been pretty specific about their requirements: they need someone who has worked for a small IT solutions company with four areas of experience – these are essential (without these they would not consider the candidate).
>
> I set these 'essential characteristics' out pretty clearly in the advert, they were:-

Leadership – Managing a team of around 15 staff, between 10 and 12 of whom will be field based; organising and motivating the team to ensure the 'face of IT' is functioning well; and delivering first class service.

Service Delivery – The company operates in a competitive niche where they've carved out a great reputation and compete with much larger organisations. The way they've done this is through the quality of their service. As they expand, they need to continue and improve upon this service, and they need someone who can implement improvements and structures.

Client Management – Someone to get very close to their clients, building great relationships to understand their business; identifying any issues in advance, retaining their business, and ultimately expanding and developing the services being provided.

Project Management – Working closely with the business to deliver multiple projects on time and against budget; understanding what can be done (and also what can't.). This is project management for someone who has managed large numbers (dozens) of small projects at any one time—often only 1 week projects—rather than someone who is experienced at managing large global projects.

I also made the point that it would be a real advantage to set out in a covering letter where there was a match in experience. We had 979 unique applications for this role. How many covering letters addressed these points? 1! Yes, only one candidate.

Now, maybe I should call every candidate to discuss the role in detail, but I didn't, nobody would, it's impossible. Is this fair? Probably not. Is it reality today? Yes.

Was he the best candidate for the job? Yes, I think so. Among the 979 candidates, were there plenty of others who could have done a good job? I suspect so.

The point here is: Personalise your cover letters, writing a fresh one every time for every job. Look at the requirements, think about how you match them, and set this out in straightforward, normal, language in an email. Most people can't be bothered. They either don't write covering letters at all, or they have 'standard' cover letters that they kid themselves are tailored for the specific role because they've changed the job title and done a bit of 'topping and tailing'.

Granted, it takes a lot more work, but what do you think will lead to getting the right job, sending out 300 applications (or applying for the same job over and over again) or writing specific applications setting out very clearly how you match the requirements?

I know which option I would be taking.

Ace Interviews EVERY Time!

In step 2, I mentioned that there are three questions every employer wants the right answers to when considering a potential employee. There are hundreds of questions an employer might ask you, but every one of these questions is, ultimately, some form or other of one of just three questions. The first one is "*can you do the job?*" The second one: "*will you enjoy doing the job (will you love the job)?*" And the third question is, "*will they love working with you?*" To get any job, you *must* be able to answer these three questions successfully.

So, every bit of preparation you do needs to be aimed at answering those three questions, again:-

1. **Can you do the job?**
2. **Will you enjoy the job?**
3. **Will they enjoy working with you?**

Bearing this in mind, there are three key aspects to the interview, I call these the three P's.

The 3 P's

➲ Preparation,
➲ Presentation, and
➲ Performance.

Preparation:

So many people—in fact, the vast majority—do not

prepare for interviews. When I say the 'vast majority', I mean 80% of all people who go along for an interview. If you don't prepare, you may as well not go along, there's absolutely no point in turning up in the first place because you will not get the job.

So, when you get the interview, prepare properly for it. It's the very, very first thing you really must do. If 80% of the people who go for an interview haven't prepared, then simply by preparing thoroughly you automatically find yourself in the 20% who have a chance of getting the job. The other 80% haven't got a hope in hell. See how important it is to prepare?

When I'm debriefing candidates after interviews, and I ask them if they've prepared, they always say "*yes*". But when I talk to the interviewer, the interviewer will always tell me that the candidate wasn't prepared. Strange, huh? How does this happen? What this means is that it's not that people can't be bothered to prepare, or think they don't need to prepare, they just don't know *how* to. If you know how to prepare, and you do prepare, then you've got a great chance of getting the job.

So, just how do you prepare for an interview? Let's look at the sorts of things you have to do to get yourself ready for the interview to give yourself the best possible chance of getting the job.

How to prepare PROPERLY for an interview:

Do your research.

The first thing you need to do when you're preparing for the interview is to think about the questions you might be asked. You can't control the questions that you will be asked but you can still prepare for those questions. You'll have a pretty good idea of what those questions are likely to be because earlier in this section we spoke about the three key facts that you've got to get over in an interview to get the job. Every question your interviewer asks you is going to be focussed on those three points. (The first few questions in an interview are 'warm-up' questions; they're intended to help everyone settle in.)

The company's website.

You can guarantee that the first question is going to be, "*what do you know about our company?*" You need to respond with a concise, intelligent summary of their business. So, have a look at the company website. This is a must because this first question is clear-cut, you will either know the answer, or you will not. There's no way you'll be able to skirt around the answer without looking foolish. You must be able to look at the website and come up with a concise summary, in 30 to 45 seconds, of what the company does.

Companies often put their own news pages on their websites publicising the things they're proud about. So, as well as looking at the company website, try to have a look at their news page. What interesting things are going on there? For example, have they had any new contract wins, attended any exhibitions, or launched any new products? Go on to Google and do some Google news searches. Are they in the news at the moment? If you do see anything interesting either on Google or on the company's news page, let them know that you've noticed and that you're impressed with it, again, this shows that you've prepared.

Use social media to find out as much background

information and news about the company as you can.

LinkedIn tells you so much information about any potential company you're going to: how many people work there; who these people are; the types of skills they've got; you can see what background the company's employees have and who else they're connected to; who's left recently and who's just joined the company? What does their Facebook page say about them? What are their offers? What are their customers saying, good and bad? What's on YouTube and Twitter about them? Are there different forums talking about what they do or their new product and how brilliant it is?

All of this research on your potential employer will pay off: It shows to the interviewer that you have anticipated their questions; it shows that you are interested in the company (that you will enjoy working there); it will help you to prepare confident and intelligent answers, and it will boost your own self-confidence.

And what does all this lead to?

➲ Making a great first impression!

Remember the 60 second rule? When the first impression you make is that of a confident and competent potential employee, you're a long way towards answering those three questions that you have to answer to get the job.

If you want some scripts that work, go to www.brightstarttraining/itpro and get access to the online training which will make sure your first impressions count, as well as some handy tips on how to ace your interview each and every time!

As well as being able to recite a 30 second spiel about the company, another good tip here is to print out a couple of pages from the company's website. Take those printouts along with you. When you get into the interview and you open up your folder and you have a couple of pages of printouts on the company, the interviewers will automatically think, *"Yes, this person has prepared and is ready to take the interview seriously."* Again, this all helps to make that all-important good first impression.

Prepare and rehearse your 'sales' pitch.

The second question in the interview is almost always going to be, *"Can you tell me a little bit about yourself."* A response to this question along the lines of, *"What would you like to know?"* will not work, it puts the interviewer on the back foot and will make them feel uncomfortable. Again, have a concise 30-45 seconds introduction as to who you are, why you're there, and what you're looking for, at the ready. You're giving a 45 second sales pitch on yourself. *Remember:* one of the things they want to know is whether *they* will enjoy working with *you*; you need to come across as a friendly, warm person, who makes them think a little bit.

There's no point my saying, *"don't be nervous when you go for an interview,"* because you *will* be nervous. Just bear in mind that you're talking about the one subject that you know better than anyone else in the world, yourself. There's nothing these people can ask you that you don't know the answer to because you know everything about yourself. But to give yourself the best chance under pressure, you need to prepare properly, you need to have thought about the types of questions you're going to be asked, and you need to be ready for those questions.

Imagine you're interviewing yourself;

If you were interviewing yourself, what would you ask? What is it about you that makes you the ideal person for the job? Where can you add value to this job? Think about these things and bring them into the answers to your questions. Think about why you would be great at this job and why they should definitely give you this job. Have the key points in mind that you want to get over.

Prepare a list of questions..

Prepare a list of questions that you want to ask the interviewer. What are great questions? A great question is one that makes the interviewer stop and think about the question you've asked and respond with you in mind. It's great if they say, *"No one has asked that before"*, or *"That's a great question."*

If you ask, *"What training is available?* "or *"What's the progression in the role?"* or *"How many days holiday do I get?"*, these are not great questions as **all of these things are about *you*.** The perception of someone asking these questions is that *it's all about you, not them*. But the company is looking to solve ***their*** problem. Yes, they want you to get the job, which potentially solves your problem, but they're looking to solve their own problem. Don't make your questions about you. Make your questions about them, but make those questions focus upon *you solving their problems*. This will make you stand out from the crowd, the majority of the other candidates will be asking the same old self-focussed questions: *"What training is available? What's the progression? How am I going to do these things?"* These are not great questions.

Let's look at some real examples of what types of questions you could ask.

> **Great questions** are questions that *you've* thought about. Again, it's about thinking for yourself, being different, and being a little bit creative.
>
> **Great question #1**; *"In six-month's time, looking back on the role, if you hire me what will I need to have done to be successful?"*
>
> **Great question #2**; *"What's the biggest challenge I will face with this role in the next three months?"*
>
> **Great question #3**; *"If I started this job tomorrow, what's the first thing I would be doing?"*

The real, real, key to this is to go away and think about your own questions. Think about what questions you're going to ask and the impression that those questions are going to make. This is your chance to leave a good impression on the hiring manager; the examples I've given above will make him or her think about you in this role.

Know your CV.

Often, the structure of the interview follows what's on

your CV. If it's on the CV, be prepared to talk about it and to expand upon it. All the interviewer knows about you is what's on your CV. Now, a lot of us wrote our CV a long time ago and don't necessarily know or remember what's on there; lots of us maybe got a little bit of help, whether from a professional CV writer, our parents, or someone we knew at college.

Know what's on your CV and be prepared to expand on all of those things.

Think about real life examples, tell a story.

Think about three or four scenarios that you've been in and give real examples of these situations when you're answering a question. These scenarios can be anything; work-based scenarios, university or college-based scenarios, or perhaps projects that you've worked on in your spare time. They can be absolutely anything but think of real examples of situations, and think about them before the interview. The reason I say this is that in an interview situation you're under pressure and your mind will go blank if you haven't thought of a few scenarios in depth beforehand. You might even make a note of them on your notepad that you take with you. The way to think of them is to think about the situation you've been in, how you dealt with it and what the outcome was (obviously, I'm talking about positive outcomes here.)

The preparation techniques we've covered in this section involve a lot of work, but this applies to any interview you go to so the good news is that you don't need to go through every single step each time you get an interview. The questions part of it will certainly be relevant for lots of jobs you go for. *But remember*: 80% of candidates don't prepare at all. And 95% of people will not have done all of the above. So, it shouldn't be too difficult to work out that if you *do* do all of the things I've covered here, you will stand a pretty good chance of getting the job.

Presentation:

Okay, research done. Answers to questions thought about. You're now ready for the interview.

How do you present yourself in an interview?

When candidates have been invited for interview, I always ask, *"What sort of message, what sort of image, are you trying to put over in this interview?"* Invariably the answer is, *"I don't know, I'm just going to go along and try and answer their questions; do my best."* That's good—we do want to be doing our best—but it's competitive out there. You want to give yourself that little bit of an edge that actually does make the difference between being hired for the job and not being hired.

Arriving at the Interview.

You need to be sitting in the reception area ten minutes before the interview starts, no earlier, no later. If you get there earlier, the interviewer is under pressure. People are busy; they might be inconvenienced. While it's important to make sure you don't get delayed and miss your interview as a result, if you do arrive earlier than ten minutes before, wait outside the office.

<u>Don't be late</u>. If you're late for the interview there are no excuses, you won't get the job. It doesn't matter whether your excuse is that the train was late, the traffic was bad, or your alarm didn't go off. None of these things matter. In my experience, 99% of people who are late for an interview do not get the job. If you're running slightly late you need to phone ahead straight away; you need to let your interviewer know straight away.

We've talked elsewhere and about first impressions, and this is a prime example: *If you can't get to the interview properly and on time then what does that say about you?*

Look smart. Still on the topic of first impressions, whenever you go for an interview in IT you need to be smart. You need to be wearing a nice suit and clean shoes; you need to have a tie on, and your top button should be fastened. You don't need to buy a hugely expensive suit for the occasion, and you should not be over-dressed. You'd be amazed how many people turn up for interviews without a tie on, with their top button undone, or with dirty shoes. If you're a woman, then you should wear something equally as smart, a business suit, over the knee skirt or dress with a tailored jacket, or trousers; nothing too revealing. And makeup should be subtle. Don't wear too much jewellery, and make sure your hair is clean and in a style that says 'professional' NOT 'nightclub.' Should this make a difference? Perhaps not, but it does. Think about how you present yourself professionally and make sure you look the part.

Be friendly. I understand you'll be feeling nervous, but be friendly to everyone as you don't know who people are. When you go into the office be especially friendly to the receptionist, she or he can have a big influence. Talk to him or her if you're sat waiting for your interview, you might find out something interesting about the company and might be able to use this in your interview. You'll certainly get a feel for what it's like to work there and whether or not it's the sort of place where you want to work. Also, even a friendly five-minute conversation with someone who isn't going to be the decider in this process doesn't half help to calm your nerves. So, be friendly to everyone.

So, you're sitting in reception. You've had your conversation with the receptionist and you're waiting for the interviewer to come out and get you. When they do come out, greet the interviewer with a firm handshake, not a limp lettuce. Make eye contact with them, smile at them and, again, be friendly. At the risk of repeating myself, *first impressions count.* Whether you believe the stats or not, the fact is they're going to make their mind up pretty quickly about whether they like you or not. These initial exchanges make the difference between it being a relaxed and successful interview and it being a tense, uncomfortable one. These people want you to get the job; they've looked at your CV and think you can do it. Everything so far has been leading up to you getting the interview. Once you've been invited, you have every chance of getting this job so use that chance wisely.

As the interviewer comes to meet you and he or she walks you through to the interview room, what are they going to do? Normally, they're going to ask you how you are. What was your journey like? Be positive. People want to work with positive people. Go back to the three points that we made earlier, one of which was; *"are you going to be a good person to work with?"* Part of that is how friendly or warm you are, or how you interact with people. So, be positive. We don't want to hear that you've been stuck on a train and you were very late, and it was a horrible journey; or you didn't sleep last night. Be positive and friendly, and don't ever mention anything negative to them.

This little walk to the interview room might also be a chance to show some of the preparation you've done. If the moment is right, mention something great about the company, perhaps a recent news article, or an award they've won. These first impressions are all very, very, important and start with these little interactions before the interview starts. They make a huge difference as to whether you're going to ultimately get the job.

Performance.

The final aspect of the three P's is performance. If you've done the right preparation and you've made a good first impression, you now have to press home that advantage. There are a couple of obvious things that you need to be doing first. You need to look at the interviewer, listen to what they're saying, and you need to try and be open and relevant with your answers. Speak clearly, and let the interviewer run the interview, as an interviewer, there's nothing worse than someone jumping in and interrupting your questions, even if that person is trying to add something. Let the interviewer finish asking their question before responding to them.

I know we've spoken about thinking of scenarios already, but make sure you answer the questions your interviewers ask. If they're asking a question, there's a reason they want to know the answer for that question. The interview is about *you* showing *them* that you can do the job, and that you want the job; that you'd be good at the job, and would love doing the job. But your interviewers also want to know whether you'd be a good person to work with, so answer the questions they ask.

We've spoken here about face-to-face interviews and the process I've outlined is the same with a telephone interview. But there are many other different types of interview: Phone interviews, competency-based interviews, panel interviews, group interviews. (We talk about competency-based interviews shortly). If you've arranged the interview through a recruiter or you've arranged it yourself, it's a good idea to ask what type of interview to expect so you'll know how they're going to conduct the interview. How are they going to structure it? Try and find out a little bit about what it's going to look like. But whatever the form of the interview, you need to keep those three important questions in mind and how you're going to answer them. *Can you do the job? Will you love doing the job? Will they love working with you?*

If you've prepared well for the interview, you will have already identified your key strengths and how they relate to the employer and how you can be of benefit to them. The interview is your chance to get this over to your future employer in the right way. Every answer you give should be aimed at doing those three things.

As well as the first impressions that we spoke about earlier, last impressions also count. At the end of the interview, you'll normally get a chance to say something. So, the interviewer will say, *"Have you got anything else for us?"* Someone once said to me, *"Thank you for taking the time to see me today. I just want to say that this is the job that I've been looking for, and if you give me the chance I guarantee I'll give it 100% and I'm certain I can be a success."* Guess what? He got the job. It was very, very powerful, and it leaves a lasting impression. I've mentioned this to lots and lots and lots of people. It takes a bit of confidence to say it, and you have to believe it and prepare it, but give it a go, it works.

All of this (the 3 Ps) involves thinking differently; it might even involve taking a risk. For example, you might feel like a bit of a prat saying, *"Thank you for taking the time to see me today,"* and so on. The majority of people won't do any of these things. Do yourself a favour and try it, it works.

Competency-based Interviews

It's definitely worth looking at competency-based interviews in a bit more depth because they're very, very, popular with both large and small companies; a lot, if not most, of interviews today will have some element of competency-based questions. So, we'll be looking at some of the types of questions that will come up and how you go about addressing them.

Competency-based interviews are designed to find out how you've performed and reacted in previous situations. The logic behind them is that how you've performed in the past is the best indication of how you'll perform in the future. So, rather than asking you what you *would* do if this type of situation came about—say, a difficult customer—they would ask, *"tell me about a time when you dealt with a difficult customer?"* Or, for an IT job, *"tell me about a time when you had a user that called who was really disappointed with the level of service and how you dealt with the situation?"*

Competency-based questions are the very, very, best

type of questions that you can hope to get. This is because they're asking about scenarios that you've been in, how you've reacted to them, and all the things that you've done.

So, you know the answers to a competency-based interview. As an aside, I've prepared a toolkit where there's a question bank of all the different types of questions you tend to find in competency-based interviews. If you go to www.brightstarttraining.com/itentrylevel, and type in your name and e-mail address, you'll be able to access the question bank there.

There are a couple of things that you need to be aware of though. You must be prepared for the questions in advance, I mentioned earlier that in an interview, without any shadow of a doubt, you're going to be very, very, nervous. If you're very, very, nervous you can't always think of things off the top of your head. But if you've thought beforehand, and prepared a number of different scenarios for these competency questions, you will generally find that if you've got three or four different scenarios they can be tailored to match lots of different situations.

So, the question of, *"Tell me about a time you were particularly proud of the service that you delivered to the customer,"* could often be the same scenario as, *"Tell me about a customer who wasn't very happy with what you've done and how you've turned it around."* You need to think about these beforehand. If you go in there blind you won't be able to think of the right examples off the top of your head. If we were chatting in the pub on a Friday night, it would be easy to talk about all of the scenarios because you'd be relaxed; but, when you're nervous, you won't be able to relax.

STAR:

How do interviewers judge the answers to competency-based interviews (or, for that matter, all interview questions)? The interviewers can be looking for negatives as well as positives. Take care in situations where the interview could be open to you not being open to change, failing to get help sooner, or even failing to get help at all. The way to answer negatives is to follow a set procedure. The acronym for this procedure is '**STAR**'.

Firstly, you think of the **Situation or the Task** that you had. Describe the situation that you were in and what you needed to do in that situation. It needs to be a specific event; you need to be talking about something that you actually did. It could be a part of your dissertation or a part of your first job; it might relate to a customer service job you had before you were looking into IT. Whatever the event, it must be specific, and it must be something that has genuinely happened; it must also be work-related. Perhaps it was when you were volunteering for something; or a project you did at school, some teamwork you did, or a particular project you worked on. (Go to the websites and have a look at the question bank for some ideas of the types of questions you might get). Explain the situation in enough detail so the interviewer can understand where you're coming from.

The A in STAR stands for Action - the action that you

specifically took. This isn't always comfortable when you're answering questions because often we'll say, *"We did this,"* or *"We did that,"* but it's not about *"we"* in these scenarios, it's about what *you* did to solve the problem. Other people might have helped in certain ways, but look at the action that you specifically took. Describe what you did in detail, and be sure to keep the focus on what you *did* (not what you might do or what you should have done). Be honest about what you did.

Then you move on to the **Results** - what happened? How did the event end? What did you accomplish? How happy was the customer at the end of it? What did you learn? Explain the **S**ituation in the **T**ask; look at the **A**ctions you specifically took, then the **R**esults. Obviously, at this stage the scenarios you're going to give are going to be scenarios that have ended positively. It might be when a customer or a user called you particularly unhappy about the service; or, perhaps their PC wasn't working or they couldn't access the website. Whatever the situation was, explain the action that you specifically took to put it right, and then at the end of it—assuming the customer was happy—say how happy the end result was and how positive your actions were.

As you're answering these questions the interviewer will follow-up with other questions, particularly if you haven't given enough detail. They might say, *"What was your specific role in this?"* They might ask what challenges you came across. Why exactly did you make that decision? How did you approach that? How did you feel? Whose idea was it? What exactly was the outcome? What would you do differently next time? These are all questions you need to be ready for, prepare the situations beforehand and then think about the types of questions you might be asked. For lots more examples of these types of question go to the question bank on the website that I've given above.

How do you know what competencies or questions they're going to ask?

It's easy, just have a look at the job description. Often it will give you a list of the competencies that you're going to need. It might say that you need to have particular skills in problem solving. Go to the question bank on the website, go to the section on problem solving, and look at the types of questions. As you're looking at those questions, you'll realise that a couple of scenarios fit them all. So, go away and think of occasions when you've had to do these things. When have you had to solve a problem? We've all had to do this; whether it was part of your degree, or part of a problem at work, we've all had to do these things. Think about them and write them all out. Don't necessarily take these along with you but just get your ideas clear and down on to paper: what the situation was, what you did, why you did it, what the outcome was, and what you learned.

Think about the follow-up questions and be prepared to expand on your answers; again, though, keep focussed on the specifics of exactly what you did.

So, STAR is pretty simple really:

- ✓ You explain the **S**ituation and **T**asks,
- ✓ the **A**ctions you specifically took,
- ✓ and then the **R**esults you achieved.

Interview X Factor

Do you have the interview *X factor*? What is the interview X factor? At the end of the day, what's going to be the deciding factor as to who is likely to get offered this job? We've looked at the three questions the interviewer is trying to get positive answers to: Can you do the job? Are you going to love the job? Are they going to love you doing the job? But if more than one candidate demonstrates positive answers to all of these questions, what determines who will get the job?

The answer is:

- **Likeability and the ability to engage with the interviewers.**

Some people reading this book will say, *"Nonsense. It's because I don't have enough experience"*. But trust me, if the person who's interviewing likes you, thinks that you want to work with them, and thinks that you're 100% committed to doing a great job, you won't need experience. They'll train you in the latest software; they'll get you up to speed on what you need to get up to speed on. Focus on that - it's about likability and engaging your interviewers.

How do you 'engage with the interviewer?'

Simple, find something out about the company that's great and let them know. Let them know that you've had a look at it. Before the interview starts, chat about non-job-related things. For example, if you notice a picture on golf in the office, and you like golf, mention it. A word of warning though, only talk about things you're genuinely interested in.

Show a little bit of *passion, a bit of personality*; show the types of things that you're interested in. Be nice, open, and friendly; make friends with people, be interested in the interviewer, and be interested in the company. Show loads of enthusiasm about the job, the company, and why you want to work there. Ask them why it's a great place to work. Ask the gentleman or lady who's interviewing, *"why do you love working for this company?"* Be interesting, be positive the whole time, smile, and keep eye contact with them.

Do these things really help you get a job? Is this really going to make a difference? Yes, absolutely. I've interviewed hundreds and hundreds of people, and have employed hundreds of people. The people you give the jobs to are the people you like. Of course, you need to prove your ability to do the job, but if an interviewer likes you and wants to work with you, you'll be surprised what they will do to get you there.

It's easy to look back over these and think; *"I do all of these things."* Okay, but how well do you do them, honestly?

Now, we all know someone who gets every job they're interviewed for, don't we? They always seem to get promoted and they always seem to be lucky. Guess what these annoying people do? They do all of these simple steps that we've talked about here. They've practiced them beforehand but they seem to do them naturally. It's these little steps that give you that interview 'X factor' that'll make you go further.

Following Up;

We've spoken about the interview, preparation, presentation, performance, and a little about how you answer questions. We've spoken about likability and the importance of that. This final part is about following up. Following-up on your interview is important, it does have an impact.

One undeniable fact today is that, for most jobs, there's enormous competition. There are lots of good candidates out there. We've spoken about ways you can deal with this competition but there will always be some level of competition. There are going to be lots of good, capable, candidates who are going to be very frustrated; they're going to be rejected and they're going to feel disappointed. There are going to be plenty of times when you come a close second; picked to the post at the last minute. Unfortunately, that's life.

You absolutely must keep yourself in the mind of the interviewer by following-up. I spoke earlier about how to make the potential employer think about you in terms of the job. Don't pester; don't harass; don't stalk people—these things are never cool—but *do* follow-up.

2 Quick ways to follow up:

1. Drop a quick **e-mail** saying that you thought the interview went well, you were pleased, and you thought you could make a difference in X, Y or Z way (talk about specifics). Follow-up and say what a great place to work it would be.

2. Perhaps drop by their offices **with a letter** saying *"I really would like the opportunity to come along*

> *and work for your company. I think I could do these types of things very well. This is my dream job, give me a chance."*

You'd be surprised how often these little follow-ups work.

➲ **Remember: differentiate yourself, be different!**

What happens if you've come second?

There was a great candidate who just picked you to the post, so you've come second. Make a diary note to follow-up on that. Whether it's a week or a fortnight, whether it's with a recruitment agency or an employer direct, make a little note to follow-up. You never know what might happen in those couple of weeks.

When you're job hunting, you're up against loads of other job seekers. Some of them are out of work; others, though, are looking for a change. After another candidate has accepted the job, and you've been told, *"Sorry, you haven't got the job"*, anything can and, trust me, does go wrong. The person who's got the job might get a better offer with another employer; they might receive an increase in salary from their existing company; another job might open up in their existing company. If any of these things happen, it isn't fair to assume that you'll be called back.

If you **follow-up**, you're showing your enthusiasm and proactivity; you're keeping yourself in view; you're showing that you want the job. You may well get a nice e-mail back saying, *"Sorry, the person who accepted the job is doing great, but thanks again"*. Nevertheless, things can change overnight.

You will never do yourself any harm by following up positively and making contact. You never know what's going to happen in these places again, and it isn't fair to assume that once you've been there for one interview you'll always be at the forefront of their minds, you won't be. Your details will get buried under a mountain of other CVs. One telephone call, one e-mail, one follow-up, all of these can result in additional interviews and even job offers. I've seen it happen. You might be re-interviewed; the process can be shortened because of your prior interviews with the company.

Going back to what we were talking about earlier around themes of networking with people, building relationships with people, and just making friends with people, it works. Granted, it takes a bit of effort but—and I've said this dozens of times—it's *worth it; it does make a difference*. The vast majority of people don't do these things.

Be creative. Be different. Be the one to stand out from the crowd.

Summary

The way of hunting for a job has changed. You need to be on top of these changes if you're going to land your dream job in IT

So remember:

- ✓ Be creative and different
- ✓ Your CV must sell
- ✓ Think about your personal brand

If you're tired of being rejected at interviews, you simply

must follow the guidelines I've provided here. Get to grips with the 3 **P's** and make sure you do your research before you go in to your interview. You have just 60 seconds to make an impression – you need to make those 60 seconds count.

Remember:

The vast majority of people have no idea about how to prepare for interviews or how to create a lasting impression, but you now know exactly what you need to do. And don't forget that once the initial interview is over, there is one more critical step to take:-

- **Follow up!**

If you take everything on board that I've said in this section, you WILL stand out from the crowd and you WILL go further in IT

SECTION 2

- **Conclusion**
- **Following the '3-Step Process'**
- **About the Author**
- **Glossary**
- **Next Steps**

SECTION 2

Conclusion

The fact that you are reading this concluding section is great news, most people will not have read this far. You should now be equipped with a vast array of tools to help you to get the best IT job ever. But you need to put the things I've talked about into practice ***today.*** It's not enough to say *"yes, good ideas; I can see how that works. I'll definitely do something about this next week when I'm less busy."* Don't be in the majority of people you will not do the things that I've shown them in this book.

When you start working on the things I've discussed in this book, you might find it difficult at first. It will require a lot of hard work. But keep in mind the end game: never having to apply for a job again, earning more money in a job you love with the flexibility to work on projects that you really enjoy, and *really* making a difference to your future career prospects.

If you're reading this book in between continual rejection and applying for hundreds of jobs, day in and day out, I'm pretty sure you'll find that putting the contents of this book into action will reap far greater rewards.

Provided you actually make time and commit to doing something that makes a difference *today,* you

will stand out and you will definitely achieve your dreams – *you will get the best IT job EVER!*

Following 'The 3-Step Process'

As I've mentioned in this book, if you follow my 3-step plan, you *will* land your dream job in IT, so long as you remain open and willing to try something different.

What I'm talking about here is that it's essential that you keep a positive mental attitude. I know that this can be very difficult, especially if rejection-after-rejection is the norm at this point in your career. The good news, though, is that my 3-step plan should actually *help* you to remain positive.

During my time in recruitment, I've heard every reason why a person is still out of work:

1. 'I didn't go to the best university' (or 'didn't go to university.')
2. 'No one will give me a chance'
3. 'I don't have any commercial experience'
4. 'It's who you know, not what you know'

Do you know what all these 'reasons' have in common?

➲ **They're all excuses!**

In terms of the extent to which these excuses are likely to hinder your success of landing that dream IT job, the worst is number 2 ('no one will give me a chance'). If you're using this excuse, you're blaming something that is *external* to you. We all externalise to some extent because doing so helps us to feel better about ourselves.

Blaming our unfortunate circumstances on others can sometimes be very helpful. For example, think of the things you said to yourself when someone you loved finished your relationship, it's very likely that you blamed the other person, rather than yourself, for that failed relationship (for example, 'he's a commitment-phobe' or 'she's selfish'). But it's *not at all* helpful to externalise when it comes to trying to land your dream job in IT because you will not be *motivated* to find that dream job.

On the other hand, once you recognise that *you* are in control of your destiny, you'll be motivated to do things that *will* help you to land your dream job.

The remaining 'excuses' involve blaming yourself (in terms of your lack of education, experience, and social connections). If any of these types of excuses ring true, then you're explaining the causes of your unfortunate circumstances in terms of your *own* shortcomings. But here's the good news: these are all things that ***you can work on***, you *can* gain more experience, you *can* train in a relevant qualification(s), and you *can* build more connections with people.

In fact, I've given you dozens of examples of how you can now 'get more experience' without having to necessarily get a job which covers your specialist area.

Using sites like LinkedIn and Twitter can make an enormous difference too. You can build great relationships with people and build up a fantastic 'online presence' which will be a huge help in your job seeking activities.

Incidentally, there are people out there who are at the top of the IT ladder, yet every one of the above 'excuses' (albeit never used as excuses) applied to them. Steve Jobs was a college dropout, Alan Sugar grew up on a council estate in Hackney and left school at age 16, Pete Cashmore set up Mashable from his bedroom at the age of 19, and Jeff Bezos started Amazon from his garage.

The difference is that these highly successful people ***did something about their difficult situations.*** They also differentiated themselves, and they 'specialised' something that, as you will now know, is critical in the current job market.

So, now you have the tools to get the IT job of your dreams. **But make sure you put these techniques into practice.** You will be in the top 0.01% of people if you do, and you will stand head and shoulders above your competitors.

I really want you to succeed. And I love hearing about people who have taken my advice on board and got their dream job. So, please do get in touch to let me know what has worked for you and how you've implemented the tactics I've outlined.

I wish you all the best for your future career!

A Bit About Me and Why I've Written This Book

I've been in the recruitment business for about twelve years and run an IT recruitment company. As a result of this experience, I've gained considerable insight into why some people land their dream IT jobs seemingly effortlessly, whereas others are still searching after months, sometimes even years, of gruelling hard work. To me, the differences between these two types of people—or, rather, the job hunting strategies they're using—are obvious. I've worked with hundreds of candidates to help them get their dream jobs in IT; I've spoken to thousands of people who have hugely successful careers in IT; and I've spoken to thousands of people who, after months or years, are still trying to land the job of their dreams.

Because of these experiences, I know what works and what doesn't work, and I can therefore help you to get your dream job—*without* going down the tedious and frustrating route of applying for every job that comes along. That is why I have developed created the online training programme (and written this book) which will allow you to be successful and get the job you want.

I've mentioned it a number of times in the book and I say it hear again, the vast majority of people that read this book will not do anything different. Even though they realise what they are doing is not working they keep on doing it. I'm not saying these people aren't trying, they are trying really hard but for whatever reason they are not prepared to **do something different**.

At this stage you've got two options, you can either put the book down, do nothing and continue to struggle or you can start to implement the ideas and principles I've outlined and if you're really smart, get access to the full online training programme which covers everything in much more detail. If you've decided to take action fantastic, implement one idea at a time, be focussed and I'm certain you will have a hugely successful career.

Want to know how to gain access to this online training programme that goes into more depth and walks you, step by step through every stage? Be warned, it's only for those of you who are serious about getting your dream job. Simply visit www.brightstarttraining.com/itpro and get instant access now.

I wish you all the best in your IT career – and look forward to hearing from you on LinkedIn.

Glossary

1st Line Support - When a user reports a problem, this is the point where the IT department first attempts to resolve the problem. Typically this will be helpdesk support and will involve basic technical support and troubleshooting.

2nd Line Support - If 1st line support cannot solve a user's problem, it is escalated to 2nd line support. More advanced support and most basic issues will be resolved at this level.

3rd Line Support – If both lower tiers cannot resolve an issue it gets escalated to third line who are typically senior and experienced technicians. Server issues are also dealt with at this level.

Android - Is a mobile operating system developed by Google and is based upon the Linux kernel and GNU software.

App - Is an abbreviation for application. An app is a piece of software. It can run on the Internet, on your computer, or on your phone or other electronic device.

App Store - Is a service for the iPhone, iPod Touch and iPad created by Apple Inc. which allows users to browse and download applications from the iTunes Store.

Blackberry - Is a smartphone that is widely used in the enterprise for its wireless email handling capability.
C# - (pronounced "C-sharp") is an object-oriented programming language from Microsoft.

Cloud Computing - The practice of using a network of remote servers hosted on the Internet to store, manage, and process data.

Commvault – Data and storage management software.

Content Management System (CMS)– Is a system used to manage the content of a Web site.

Database - A structured set of data held in a computer, esp. one that is accessible in various ways.

Helpdesk – A service that provides information and assistance to users of a computer network. Often (normally) the first point of contact.

Jobserve – Online website specialising in advertising IT roles.

Linux - An open-source version of the UNIX operating system.

Microsoft Exchange - Part of the Windows Server line of products Exchange is a collaborative software product which handles email, calendars and daily tasks.

.NET - Is both a business strategy from Microsoft and its

collection of programming support for what are known as Web services, the ability to use the Web rather than your own computer for various services.

Object-oriented programming language - Object-oriented programming (OOP) is a programming language model organised around "objects" rather than "actions" and data rather than logic.

PHP - general-purpose scripting language that was originally designed for web development to produce dynamic web pages.

Relational Database - A database structured to recognise relations between stored items of information.

Ruby on Rails - often shortened to Rails or RoR, is an open source web application framework for the Ruby programming language.

SAN - (Storage Area Network) A network of storage disks.

Server rooms - A server room is a room that houses mainly computer servers. In information technology circles, the term is generally used for smaller arrangements of servers; larger groups of servers are housed in data centers.

SmartPhone - A smartphone is a mobile phone that offers more advanced computing ability and connectivity than a contemporary basic 'feature phone.

Software Developer / Programmer - A programmer, computer programmer or coder is someone who writes computer software.

SQL - Structured Query Language, an international standard for database manipulation.

Storage - The retention of retrievable data on a computer or other electronic system; memory.

Unix - A widely used multiuser operating system.

Virtualise - To run a program in virtual storage; To simulate (or make virtual) some effect or condition on a computer. There are a number of virtual products, the most popular of which is VMware.

Webinar – Seminar conducted over the internet.

WordPress - is an open source CMS, often used as a blog publishing application powered by PHP and MySQL. It has many features including a plugin architecture and a templating system. Used by over 12% of the 1,000,000 biggest websites, WordPress is the most popular CMS in use today.

Next Steps

Are you *serious* about getting a career in IT?

Then you need to sign up to my latest online training programme, called 'IT Professional Programme'

This revolutionary step-by-step training programme has been put together in bite sized chunks - with me walking you through each piece - so you can immediately apply what you're learning and put it to use TODAY!

The system covers the full cycle of what you need to secure a Professional Career in IT. (Imagine never having to suffer the rejection of applying for hundreds of jobs and getting no response again!)

Are you frustrated at spending months (years?) looking for work before finding a short-term contract before the whole cycle starts again? If so, and you are prepared to be open to new ideas, then this programme is a must, it shows you how to start your success journey.

The programme is a series of online videos and covers:

✓ How to identify the RIGHT Career path in IT

- ✓ Why you need to SPECIALISE! (The key to earning more and being in demand.)
- ✓ How To DIFFERENTIATE Yourself From The Competition and distinguish yourself in a tough marketplace.
- ✓ CV writing strategies that every employer wants to read.
- ✓ The 60 Second rule to gaining a competitive advantage - SCRIPTS & STRATEGIES THAT WORK!
- ✓ Learn how to gather critical information which enables you to be seen and ATTRACT offers.
- ✓ Little known job hunting strategies (that are NOT covered in the book)!
- ✓ Email shortcuts to ATTRACT INTERVIEWS AND OFFERS.
- ✓ Leverage SOCIAL MEDIA– and how to develop your social media strategy.
- ✓ LINKEDIN secrets to success (and learn the power of this networking site!)
- ✓ Using Social Media to IDENTIFY REAL TIME JOB OPPORTUNITIES (that no one else is using)!
- ✓ How to put yourself in a state of peak performance;

5 STRATEGIES FOR REMAINING FOCUSED.

This online course is usually £99 but as a thank you for buying the book *I'm making this available to you for better than half price, just £47!* However this programme will not stay at this price for long. In fact after the first 1,000 members, the price will revert back to the full £99.

Don't let this special offer pass you by. ACT NOW. I'm expecting a high sign up rate, and I would really like for you to take advantage of this special discount.

Go to www.brightstarttraining.com/itpro and follow the online instructions. Please email the team if you have any questions about the programme at theteam@brightstarttraining.com and we will be happy to help.

Richard

Don't let this opportunity pass you by - sign up TODAY!

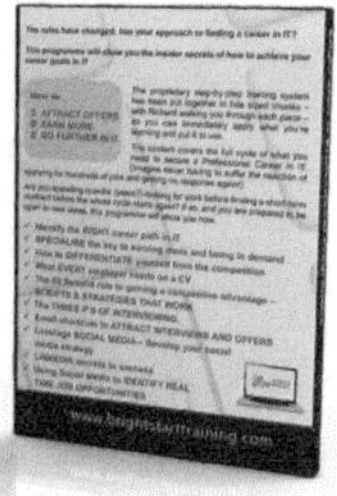